Tools of Navigation

A Kid's Guide *to the* History & Science *of* Finding Your Way

15 Hands-On Activities

Rachel Dickinson

nomad press

Nomad Press

A division of Nomad Communications

10 9 8 7 6 5 4 3 2

Copyright © 2005 by Nomad Press

All rights reserved.

ISBN: 0-9749344-0-2

Questions regarding the ordering of this book should be addressed to

Independent Publishers Group

814 N. Franklin St.

Chicago, IL 60610

www.ipgbook.com

Nomad Press

2456 Christian St.

White River Junction, VT 05001

www.nomadpress.net

Photo Credits

Pg. 16: Tower: Catherine Yen; **Pg. 27:** Spices: www.davestravelcorner.com/photos/Peru/; **Pg. 29:** Grail: www.oraculartree.com; **Pg. 30:** MarcoPolo: www.askasia.org; **Pg. 45:** Ptolemy map: www.mlahanas.de; **Pg. 47:** Columbus: http://academic.brooklyn.cuny.edu; **Pg. 48:** Poets: www.gutenberg.org; **Pg. 50:** French Astrolabe Richard Paselk, Humboldt State University, **Pg 55:** Ekertequal.www.geography.ccsu.edu; **Pg. 58:** Cook: www.plantexplorers.com; **Pg. 63:** Titanic Sinking: www.materials.unsw.edu.au; **Pg. 68:** Palmyra-jungle: www.uscg.mil; **Pg. 68:** Eureka Dunes.tif: Lee Bennett www.perrochon.com/photo/Dunes/; **Pg. 70:** Buck Farm Canyon: www.wedgie.org, Cape_cod: www.terc.edu, Panam: Image Courtesy SRTM Team NASA/JPL/NIMA http://earthobservatory.nasa.gov; **Pg. 71:** Volcano: www.familycrisp.com/montserrat.htm; **Pg. 72:** Dewey Mountain.: http://www.saranaclake.com/gallery.shtml - Courtesy of Dave Freeman and the Saranac Lake Area Chamber of Commerce; **Pg. 75:** www.archives.gov; **Pg. 75** Oregon trail: www.lib.utexas.edu/maps—Line of Original Emigration to the Pacific Northwest Commonly Known as the Old Oregon Trail from The Ox Team or the Old Oregon Trail 1852–1906 by Ezra Meeker. Fourth Edition 1907.; **Pg. 76:** Independence Rock: www.canvocta.org; **Pg. 81:** Great falls: http://lewisandclarkjournals.unl.edu; **Pg. 88:** Colorado River: http://nathancheng.com; Cliffs, Grand Canyon, Colorado: www.teridanielsbooks.com; **Pg. 92:** Everest: www.angelfire.com; **Pg. 95:** Theb: The National Oceanic and Atmospheric Administration; **Pg. 96:** Fram.: www.sverdrup2000.org/; **Pg. 97:** Proposedroutemap: http://ku-prism.org; **Pg. 98:** The PEARY: The National Oceanic and Atmospheric Administration/Department of Commerce; **Pg. 98:** Peary2. www.americaslibrary.gov/; **Pg. 102:** Magnorp: http://geo.phys.uit.no; **Pg. 103:** Shackleton—Emily Slatten www.Framheim.com, Endurance, http://home.ict.nl; **Pg. 110:** Foucault: www-obs.cnrs-mrs.fr; **Pg. 110:** Marietta Gyro: http://physics.kenyon.edu , Mobile Launcher: Rocket image—Richard d. Maurer http://www.constable.ca/v2.htm, *Technology in War—Kenneth Macksey*; **Pg. 113:** V207: www.zamandayolculuk.com/cetinbal/V2RROCKET.htm; Sputnik asm: http://nssdc.gsfc.nasa.gov/database; **Pg. 114:** Moonflag: www.hq.nasa.gov/office/pao/History/alsj/alsj-usflag.html; **Pg. 117:** UTM world.1.5: www.farmworks.com/support/utmmaps.html; **Pg. 121:** 1966 Texaco Texas Legend: www.lib.utexas.edu/maps/county_outline.html; **Pg. 122:** 0000019b: Library of congress

CONTENTS

ACTIVITIES

DEDICATION

To my husband, Tim Gallagher, and my children, Railey, Clara, Jack, and Gwendolyn.

ACKNOWLEDGMENTS

A special thank you to Lauri Berkenkamp, my editor at Nomad Press.

INTRODUCTION
NAVIGATION AS ART AND SCIENCE

Navigation is the art and science of maneuvering safely and efficiently from one point to another. The word navigation comes from the Latin *navis*, which means boat, and *agire*, which means guide, so traditionally navigation referred to the ability to guide ships from one place to another. Today we use the term navigate whenever anyone wants or needs to

navigate—
from the Latin *navis*, which means boat, and *agire*, meaning to guide.

go anywhere by any means. A hiker navigates through the woods. A navigator in an airplane gets us from one place to the next by way of the sky. A kayaker navigates his way through the mangrove swamp. Your mother navigates to the store when she drives to town to buy groceries. Anytime anyone needs to get from one point to another point, they are navigating.

In this book we're going to look at the history and practice of navigation starting way back in time. In the first chapter we'll look at examples of how and why people many, many thousands of years ago made their way from one place to another—whether by sailing from one island to another or because they were chasing mammoths across a land bridge that linked two continents.

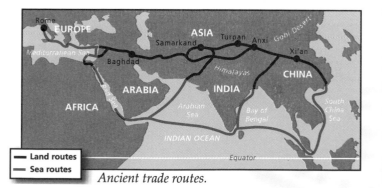

Ancient trade routes.

Then we'll look at some of the earliest trade routes—like the Spice Route between India and Egypt, the trade routes across the Mediterranean Sea, and the Silk Road that linked China to Europe. How did merchants know how to get where they wanted to go? Was it dangerous? Were they traveling by land or by sea? We'll answer these questions and take a closer look at Polynesian navigation of Oceania, and the remarkable Marco Polo and his travels.

Some key technological advances were necessary before maritime explorers could open up the wonders of the world for the rest of us. We'll develop a working understanding of several nautical instruments like the sounding line, the astrolabe, the sextant, the compass, and the chronometer. Then we'll learn how understanding and being able to measure latitude and longitude opened up exploration on the seas. We'll take a look at nautical charts and maps as well as Viking navigation, Gustavas Mercator, Magellan, Columbus, John Harrison, and Captain Cook.

After a short lesson in basic geography, which often determines why people choose to settle in one area over another, we'll discover the American West of the early 1800s, the explorations of Lewis and Clark, and subsequent efforts to open up the country to settlement. We'll take a trip through the Grand Canyon with John Wesley Powell, wander through the jungles of Africa with David Livingstone and Henry Morton Stanley, climb the world's highest peak with Edmund Hillary and Tenzing Norgay, and explore the Arctic and Antarctic with Amundsen, Peary, Scott, and Shackleton.

The twentieth century brings about aeronautical navigation and the race for space. At the same time, the development of the Global Positioning System (GPS) has made the world seem a little smaller. We'll look at these space-age developments and try to get a basic understanding of how these technologies work.

Finally, you'll learn how to put some navigational skills to work, like how to use a basic orienteering compass and read topographic and road maps. You'll actually learn how to read maps and answer questions like: What do all those little squiggly lines mean on a topographic map? Then it's time to head outside and put your newfound knowledge to work.

ICE AGE NAVIGATORS
FROM THE BERING STRAIT TO THE AMERICAS

Try to imagine how North America looked 20,000 years ago. Huge glaciers several miles thick covered all of the northern part of the continent and fingers of ice dipped far south of the Great Lakes. The sea level was almost 400 feet lower than it is today because seawater became trapped in the great ice sheets. Where not covered with ice, vast expanses of the current continental shelf were exposed.

Scientists have determined that the glaciers and vast ice sheets that covered much of North America for thousands of years began melting and receding about 18,000 years ago and by 12,000 years ago had retreated to the northern part of the continent. This opened what's known as the Bering Strait land bridge that connected the continents of North America and Asia, creating a possible migration corridor between continents for people and animals.

Learn how climate and geography influenced migration

Explore the possible routes from Asia to North America

Find out why people migrate from one place to another

What two continents did the Bering Strait land bridge connect?

There is no evidence of humans living in North America prior to 11,500 years ago. Artifacts like paintings and etchings in caves, stone tools, and bones tell us that humans lived in Europe at least 35,000 years ago alongside animals like cave bears, horses, bison, cave lions, mammoths, and rhinos. The question is—where did the first people in North America come from and how did they get here? Archeologists have been trying to piece together that puzzle for almost a century.

In the 1930s archaeologists working near Clovis, New Mexico, uncovered the remains of mastodons with stone projectiles (spear points) mixed in with the bones, indicating the animals had been killed on that spot. These projectiles,

Ice Age Starts Today

The Ancient Times Herald

Winter Weather Approaches
Experts Warn of Global Chilling

Lorem ipsum dolor sit amet, conse ctetuer adipiscing elit, sed diam no nummy nibh euismod tincidunt ut la oreet dolore magna aliquam erat vo lutpat. Ut wisi enim ad minim venia m, quis nostrud exerci tation ullamc orper suscipit lobortis nisl ut aliquip

Herds Move South

Lorem ipsum dolor sit amet, conse ctetuer adipiscing elit, sed diam no nummy nibh euismod tincidunt ut la oreet dolore magna aliquam erat vo lutpat. Ut wisi enim ad minim venia m, quis nostrud exerci tation ullamc orper suscipit lobortis nisl ut aliquip ex ea commodo consequat. Duis autem vel eum iriure dolor in hendre

FOOD DURING THE ICE AGE

Try to imagine stalking and then trying to kill an animal as big as an elephant using a stick with a stone point lashed to the end. Mammoths and mastodons were roaming North America during the last Ice Age and were an attractive food source for early people—one animal could feed many people until the meat spoiled (remember, there were no refrigerators in those days). A common hunting technique used was for a group of hunters to drive an old, injured, or very young animal into a bog or swamp and spear it to death. This could be very dangerous because the hunters had to be close to the trapped animal. Archeologists are trying to figure out if these hunters caused the extinction of mastadons.

WORDS TO KNOW

mastodon: *extinct plant-eating animal that resembled modern elphants. They were furry and about 9 feet tall, with tusks over 15 feet long.*

Clovis points: *spear points with extremely fine, sharp points found near Clovis, New Mexico.*

Clovis points.

which were stone points that would have been fixed to the ends of sticks to be used as spears, became known as Clovis points (named after the place where they were first found). Clovis points were distinctive because the stone (usually flint or chert) was fashioned in a very specific way to create extremely fine, sharp edges. In the succeeding decades, more and more Clovis points were found around North America, but oddly, no human remains were ever associated with these finds.

What became known as the Clovis-First Theory—meaning the people who used Clovis points came to America first—says that when the land bridge opened at the Bering Strait about 12,000 years ago, some Asian people made their way across the 55 miles that separates the Asian and the North American continents. Why would these early people make this journey? Because they were nomadic, big-game hunters who were following mastodons and mammoths that were also traveling along the land bridge, possibly in search of food.

This land bridge was not really like what we think of as a bridge. It was 55 miles across and up to 1,000 miles wide at points. Look at a modern-day map and you'll see just how close the farthest western point of Alaska is to the farthest eastern point of Siberia. The land bridge was in the area between the two points that is currently under water.

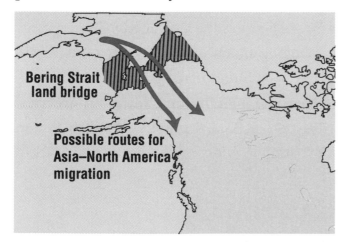

Bering Strait land bridge

Possible routes for Asia–North America migration

The Clovis-First Theory says that once in North America, people quickly spread south, eventually making their way down through modern-day Mexico and then through the Isthmus of Panama and finally into South America. How do we know this? Because

5

How did Clovis points get their name?

ICE AGE ANIMALS IN NORTH AMERICA

When the first people came to North America they found a land populated with many animals we wouldn't recognize today. These weren't dinosaurs (remember, they died out 65 million years ago) but were animals like mastodons, wooly mammoths, saber-tooth cats, giant ground sloths, short-faced bear, big-horned bison, the American lion, horses, oxen, and camels. Nearly all the large mammals of Ice Age North America became extinct in the space of 1,000 years, perhaps due to massive climate change and the arrival of people. Horses were reintroduced to the New World by the Spanish.

archaeologists have discovered the remnants of some very early settlements in South America.

A problem with the Clovis-First Theory is that once the hunters reached North America, the migration routes south through the continent were very limited. The Bering Strait land bridge—an area that scientists call Beringia—would have been like the tundra. It was a very cold, dry region that didn't support much plant life. Once early migrants made their way through Alaska, they had two possible routes into the southern portions of the continent. One was by way of the Pacific coast and the other was along the eastern flank of the Rocky Mountains. Other routes would have still been blocked by massive ice fields and glaciers.

Another problem with the Clovis-First Theory is the lack of any Clovis points in Alaska or the Bering Strait area or along much of the available migration routes. And not a single Clovis point has been found in northeastern Asia.

There are other theories about how people initially came to North America. One theory that's gaining in popularity says that Asians, possibly the early Jomon people of Japan, who already had a maritime culture, made their way to North

WORDS TO KNOW

North Pacific Rim: *the countries bordering the North Pacific, including Japan, China, North and South Korea, Russia, Canada, and the United States.*

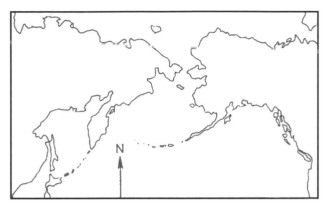

The North Pacific Rim.

America by sea. It's possible they began to migrate around 15,000 years ago and basically hopped from island to island along the North Pacific Rim (look at a map and notice where the land masses and islands are in the North Pacific). It's believed that these early seagoing peoples guided their rafts or skin boats while drifting on currents or being blown by the wind.

Perhaps the first time someone reached another island it was a mistake, for example, a fisherman who was blown off-course or caught in a storm. But when the fisherman made it back to his home he knew it was possible to make the journey. Once people knew there was land beyond their settlement, they could make a decision to travel to it.

Why would anyone want to leave their home? Assuming these are coastal people, they would want to leave once the natural resources of an area—like shellfish or marine mammals that they would have eaten or driftwood that they depended on for fuel for fires—were depleted. Coastal people who decided to travel by water had far greater mobility than people who were on foot hunting big game as they walked along the Bering Strait land bridge. They could go much farther in a shorter period of time if traveling by sea.

British Columbia.

Like the Clovis-First Theory, the theory of Asians coming by sea is not without its problems. Any theory about who originally came to America is tough to test. In this case, what would have been coastal villages or encampments of people who migrated tens of thousands of years ago now lie almost 400 feet beneath the sea. Underwater archaeologists have made some interesting

Where were the Jomon people from?

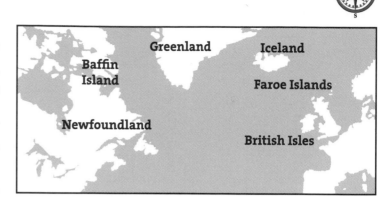

finds of artifacts off the coast of British Columbia, Canada, and around Prince of Wales Island and the Queen Charlotte Islands. However, in order to really test this theory, the technology required for this kind of underwater archeology has to be refined and further developed. At the moment, recovery of these kinds of artifacts is very, very expensive.

There is a third theory. There are archaeologists who believe the first North Americans arrived by boat but came across the North Atlantic from Europe. They base their theory on similarities between the Clovis points found in North America and Solutrean artifacts found in France. One problem with this theory is that the Solutrean culture ended more than 16,500 years ago and the earliest Clovis site dates to 11,500 years ago—that leaves a 5,000-year gap. It's possible that these early people could have island hopped across the North Atlantic (look at your modern map and notice the placement of the British Isles, Faroe Islands, Iceland, Greenland, Baffin Island, and Newfoundland), but the frigid climate and the extent of the ice during the late Ice Age would certainly have conspired against their success.

Perhaps all of these theories are correct. Archaelogists have found evidence to support all of them, and accepting one idea doesn't mean the others can't be true as well. People may have migrated to North and South America by a variety of routes from both Asia and Europe—maybe even from Australia and Africa. Some could have come by boat and others by foot. Once they were here they migrated north and south, east and west. What did every person have in common? They navigated their way, whether by land or by sea.

WORDS TO KNOW

archeology: *the study of human cultures through artifacts, human remains, and landscapes.*
ice age: *intervals of time when large areas of the globe are covered in ice. The Great Ice Age was the last major ice age in North America and Eurasia.*

ANCIENT NAVIGATORS

BRAVING THE SEA WITHOUT A COMPASS

Why would ancient people want to travel to other settlements? Think about why you go to the next town. It's often because that town has something in it that you want—either people (friends or relatives) to visit, things to buy, or places to see. Early navigators were also probably early traders. They filled their canoes, boats, and later, wagons, with goods from their villages, which they traded for goods from other settlements. What occurred along with the transfer of goods—like metals, weapons, spices, and textiles—was a transfer of ideas. Early traders discovered what was important to other cultures—they learned about their accomplishments, art, and technological innovations—and these ideas spread along trade routes.

Goods for Trade — metals, weapons, spices, and textiles

Learn how early navigators used the sun and the stars

Explore the night sky

Learn the constellations and make a sky chart

Trace the ancient, legendary trade routes and meet Marco Polo

Which lines of navigation run parallel to each other?

How did ancient people know how to navigate on the water? How could they get where they were going? There were no compasses, no maps like we think of maps, just great open expanses of water. The sea has no guiding landmarks, unlike land where travelers can follow instructions like "turn left at the big oak tree by the fork in the stream" or "head toward the mountain that looks like the head of a cow." People feared that once they got out on the water, out of sight of land, they'd never be able to find their way back home.

People around the world had different ways of getting where they wanted to go on the water. For example, experienced early mariners knew that if they sailed in a certain direction for a certain period of time they would find their destination. They could figure out their north-south orientation by observing the maximum height of the sun during the day and the maximum height of the North Star (also known as the polestar or Polaris) at night. This would determine latitude—what we think of as invisible parallel

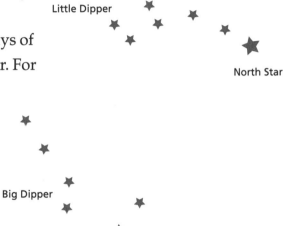

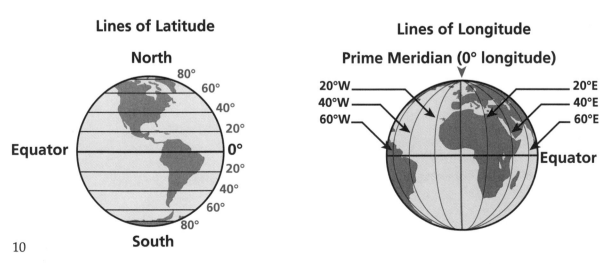

lines that encircle the earth. As long as they kept on their course and made sure that the sun or the North Star remained at the same angle in the sky when they reached their zenith, mariners could be pretty sure they were traveling due east or due west. This could be of enormous help if they knew the latitude of their home port.

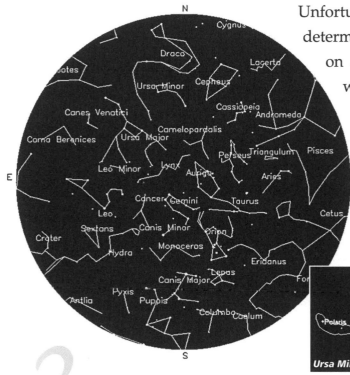

Unfortunately, ancient sailors had no way of determining longitude, or where they were on an east-west line. Longitude is what we think of as invisible lines that run north–south around the earth. These lines converge, or meet, at the North and South Poles. Think of a peeled orange and imagine that the orange is like the globe—where the individual sections come together

Ursa Minor—the Little Bear

Ursa Major—the Great Bear

WORDS TO KNOW

latitude: *east-west parallel lines that encircle the earth north and south of the equator.*

zenith: *the highest point reached in the heavens by the sun, moon, or a star.*

longitude: *north-south lines that converge at the North and South Poles and are measured in degrees east and west of the prime meridian.*

prime meridian: *the starting point for reckoning longitude; passes through the original site of the Royal Observatory at Greenwich, England.*

Ursa Major: *the most conspicuous of the constellations in the northern sky. It is near the North Pole and contains 53 visible stars, seven of which form the Big Dipper. Also called the Great Bear.*

Ursa Minor: *one of the northernmost constellations. It contains 23 visible stars, including those forming the Little Dipper. The most important of these stars is Polaris, the North Star. Also called the Little Bear.*

How did early navigators determine the distance they had traveled?

looks like what the lines of longitude would look like if they were drawn on the earth. In order to figure out exactly where they were while traveling along a line of latitude, sailors had to have an extremely accurate way of keeping track of time at sea—they would have to be able to figure out how far they traveled and how much time it took to travel that distance. Clocks of that day were worthless at sea because the rocking of the boat would make them stop. Navigators wouldn't be able to figure out longitude with any accuracy until the late eighteenth century and the invention of the chronometer (a very, very accurate clock) by the English clockmaker, John Harrison.

Without knowledge of how to determine longitude, early sailors used a system called "dead reckoning" to estimate how far east or west of a certain point they were. This required knowing the speed of the ship when it was moving and how long it took to reach any given point. Dead reckoning is still used today, although our methods of determining speed and time have greatly improved.

DEAD RECKONING

Dead reckoning is dependant on being able to make continuous measurements of course and distance traveled. A navigator starts at a known point, perhaps a port, and then measures his course and distance from that point on a chart. Course is measured by magnetic compass and distance is determined by the speed of the vessel multiplied by the time traveled.

Navigators, like Christopher Columbus, made these measurements and noted them in the ship's log (the journal of the journey). Dead reckoning does not rely on celestial navigation—you don't have to know your stars to measure distance and time. Dead reckoning was originally written in logs as "ded. Reckoning" so some think this was an abbreviation for "deduced reckoning." However, the Oxford English Dictionary thinks the word is "dead" as in "completely" or "absolutely." A dead reckoning position is one based completely on reckoning—or calculation.

WORDS TO KNOW

nautical: *relating to the sea.*

calibrated: *marked with or divided into intervals for measuring.*

CHIP LOG

A chip log was a device that sailors used to measure speed. Chip refers to a "chip of wood" and log refers to the book where these kinds of details were recorded. The wood was wedge-shaped and measured about 18 inches long. It was tied to a rope that was on a large spool at the back of the boat. The rope was knotted every 47 feet, 3 inches. One sailor threw the wood overboard while another turned over a sandglass that had 30 seconds worth of sand in it. As the boat moved away from the wood (which would catch in the water because of its shape), the rope spun off the spool. A third sailor counted the knots that passed over the rail. When the 30 seconds was up, the knot counting stopped.

The faster the ship was moving, the greater the length of rope that played out, and therefore the more knots that were counted. The space between knots was precisely the amount of rope that would play out in 30 seconds if the boat was moving one nautical mile per hour. So the number of knots counted in the 30 seconds was equal to the speed of the ship in nautical miles per hour. For example, if a sailor felt five knots slip through his hand in 30 seconds, the ship's speed would be 5 knots, which means it would cover five nautical miles in an hour if it maintained that speed. A nautical mile is 6,080 feet. A land mile is 5,280 feet.

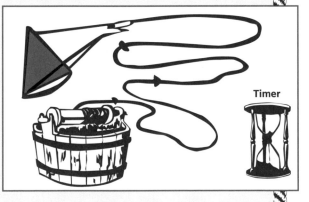

Timer

Why did they use 47 feet and 3 inches between knots on the rope and 30 seconds for the time? The length was based on converting one nautical mile per hour to feet per second, and then multiplying feet per second by 30 seconds, which was a practical time to spend counting knots with a sandglass. The result was the calibrated length in feet at which to tie the knots for a 30-second run of the chip log.

How many feet in a nautical mile? Is that greater or less than a land mile?

ACTIVITY

Learn the Constellations and Make a Sky Chart

Early explorers used the stars to find their way. We've lost touch with this skill. In this activity you will need to find a good place to observe the night sky—it's tough to see the stars if you're in a city because of the lights.

Instructions:

- Study the sky chart on page 11 of the evening sky in Central Park, New York City for July 2005.
- Think about these questions: Why does knowing the month and year on a sky chart make a difference? Why isn't this sky chart for the entire sky (Northern and Southern Hemisphere)?
- Go out at night and compare the sky chart you have with the position of the stars above you. What's different?
- The constellations have wonderful names like Pegasus (the flying horse) and Draco (the Dragon). Learn the names of the constellations and find out what they mean. Do the constellations look like their names? For example, does the Pegasus constellation look like a flying horse? Use your imagination. Can you figure out how they got these names?
- Locate the North Star or Polaris on the sky chart. It's at the end of the Little Dipper's handle. Polaris also lines up with the two stars that make the outside of the dipper of the Big Dipper. This is the most important star in navigation. Think about how generations of explorers and navigators felt safe and sure about their course after locating the North Star.
- You can make a sky chart for any time of the year and any location at **www.fourmilab.ch/yoursky**. Click "make a sky map" and then set for nearby city. This interactive web site has many options that allow you to create as simple or as complicated a sky chart as you like. To start, turn off all the display options except for constellation outlines and names. Play around with the magnitude of stars shown. At 4.0 the constellations really stand out.

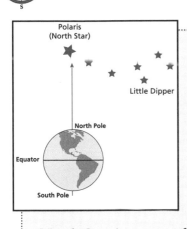

POLARIS

If you drew a line through the earth that ran through the South Pole and the North Pole and then extended it on up into the sky, you would almost hit a very bright star. This is called the North Star, or Polaris (from the word pole). Although people talk about Polaris being the brightest star in the sky, it's actually the 49th brightest star. The North Star is easy to find and has kept many travelers on course.

Early navigators determined distance traveled by multiplying the time underway (or how long they had been sailing) by the speed of the vessel. To do this, navigators used a chip log. Time was often measured with a sandglass (what we might call an hourglass) and speed was estimated by throwing a piece of wood off the stern and counting knots tied in a rope that was tied to the log. You can imagine the wild inaccuracies of this system. Think about what a floating object like a piece of wood would do if the seas were choppy. Guesses, even educated guesses, could often be way off.

So how did sailors know where they were going? They often used the stars. The ancient Egyptians recognized 36 constellations or individual stars along the ecliptic, an imaginary arc in the sky along which the sun travels during the day (the sun rises in the east and sets in the west and travels along a particular path each day of the year). Because the earth turns on its axis as it revolves around the sun (although the Egyptians didn't know this), the sun and these stars appear to move in the sky, always following the same path during the same time of year. Additionally, the stars appeared to rotate around a fixed star—Polaris—and ancient navigators knew how to find the North Star in the sky. It's easier to imagine this if you think of the night sky as being painted on the inside of a gigantic bowl that turns. The Egyptians figured out that they could map these stars or constellations and create a star clock.

WORDS TO KNOW

ecliptic: *the sun's annual path or orbit.*

Where would the North Star appear in the sky if you were standing at the geographic North Pole?

Egypt's astronomers were the first to figure out that latitude made a difference in how high in the sky a given star or constellation would appear. For example, as a person traveled north, the North Star appeared to be higher and higher in the sky. When you are at the geographic North Pole, the North Star is directly overhead. The knowledge of where the stars were at any time during the night and in any season of the year gave Egyptian sailors the ability to estimate their ship's position by making a simple measurement. Several thousand years ago, it was impossible to accurately calculate time, so latitude was an approximation (and longitude was almost impossible to determine). Nonetheless, these calculations were still enormously useful in navigation, particularly for sailors traveling a north-south route.

Ancient Wind Rose.

Egyptian sailors determined their approximate direction by tracing the path of the sun along its ecliptic. South was determined by the location of the sun when it was at its highest point, and they knew that north was in the opposite direction, and east and west were where the sun rose and set. At night, sailors steered by the stars. With knowledge of the constellations and the position of the North Star, they could keep their bearings. What did ancient sailors do when clouds obscured the sun or the stars? Very simply, they stayed off the water. For this reason there was a season for sailing, and throughout ancient times, the seas were essentially closed to navigation in winter when it was likely to be cloudy.

Ancient sailors came to rely upon their knowledge of wind and ocean currents. They noticed that winds seemed to blow from particular directions—that there were prevailing winds (not

The Tower of the Winds.

NAMED WINDS

You can find examples of named winds from all around the world. The following list shows that many cultures like to give their winds colorful names.

Roaring Forties—*Very strong westerly winds that blow almost continuously in the Southern Hemisphere. They're found at a latitude of 40 degrees—hence their name!*

White Squall—*A sudden, strong gust of wind usually seen as a whirlwind in clear weather in the tropics. It comes up without warning, and is noted by whitecaps or white, broken water.*

Squamish—*A strong and often violent wind occurring in many of the northeast–southwest or east-west running fjords of British Columbia where cold polar air can be funneled. These winds lose their strength when free of the confining fjords and are not noticeable 15 to 20 miles offshore.*

Maestro—*A northwesterly wind found in the Adriatic Sea that's associated with fine summer weather. It's most frequent on the western shore.*

Santa Ana—*A strong, hot, dry wind blowing out into San Pedro Channel from the southern California desert through Santa Ana Pass.*

Nor'easter—*A particularly strong northeast wind or gale, or an unusually strong storm preceded by northeast winds off the coast of New England—also called a Northeaster.*

Elephanta—*A strong southerly or southeasterly wind that blows on the Malabar coast of India during September and October and marks the end of the southwest monsoon.*

Cordonazo—*Also known as the "Lash of St. Francis," these are southerly hurricane winds along the west coast of Mexico. It is associated with tropical cyclones in the southeastern North Pacific Ocean. Although these storms may occur from May to November, they affect the coastal areas most severely near or after October 4, which is the Feast of St. Francis.*

Harmattan—*This is the name of the dry, dusty trade wind blowing off the Sahara Desert across the Gulf of Guinea and the Cape Verde Islands. It's also sometimes called the "Doctor" because of its supposed healthful properties.*

Mistral—*This is a cold, dry wind blowing from the north over the northwest coast of the Mediterranean Sea, particularly over the Gulf of Lions.*

In what way could a crystal, such as calcite, be used to help the Vikings navigate on cloudy days?

just gusts) that weren't random. Consequently, if a wind was blowing from your town toward another major trading port, that would be the time to set sail. These winds became known as trade winds (winds favorable for trading). Early sailors gave the winds names and described their attributes. For example, a wind coming from the southeast might always be a moist wind, whereas one that blew from the northeast might be associated with hot, dry weather. When they put these named winds down on paper (or carved them into stone) it created a wind rose, which looks something like the points of a compass.

The earliest examples of a wind rose are found in ancient Greece. For example, the eight-sided Tower of the Winds, which stands in Athens, Greece, and was built by the second-century-BCE astronomer Andronicus of Macedonia. Each side of the Tower of the Winds has a picture carved into it depicting a man representing a named wind. The name of the wind is carved along the top of the wall. In ancient Greece, sailing directions were more strongly associated with the direction and force of the prevailing winds than with the sun or stars. If a sailor had knowledge of these prevailing winds and their characteristics then he could go out to sea with some confidence that he would be able to stay on a particular bearing. Ptolemy II, king of Egypt in 250 BCE, added four more winds to the wind rose, creating the 12-point wind rose that was used throughout classical antiquity.

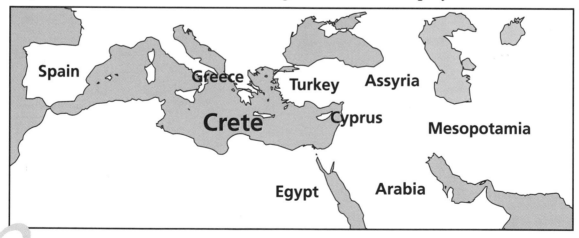

WORDS TO KNOW

BCE: *refers to before common era, a modern term for BC.*
CE: *refers to common era, a modern term for AD.*

VIKING NAVIGATION

Ancient mariners may have had an understanding of the migration patterns of birds and whales. Irish monks and Vikings (Norsemen) traveled from island to island most likely by following migrating birds. They were sailing so far north that during the summer months—or the months of the midnight sun—there would be no stars to follow for there would be no darkness at night (it was reversed in the winter months). Sailors learned to watch bird behavior. If they saw a puffin or auk flying past with a beak full of food, they knew the bird was heading back toward land and its rookery (where their baby birds were). If the beak was empty, it was heading out to sea to fish.

Atlantic puffin.

Vikings discovered Iceland around 870 CE and then Greenland about a century later. Floki Vilgjerdarsson, also known as Raven-Floki, is credited with the discovery of Iceland. He always carried a cage of ravens onboard ship. When he thought land was near, he would release one of the birds. If it circled the boat and landed back aboard, land was not near. If it flew off in a particular direction, the boat followed because they knew the bird would head toward land and food.

Many people mistakenly believe that ancient sailors hugged coastlines and stayed within sight of land because of the fear of getting lost. This doesn't seem to be true. Although there is a natural fear of the unknown and when you're out at sea you can't see any land no matter which direction you look, the greatest fear of any sailor is actually running aground or smashing against offshore reefs or underwater rocks. Chances of running aground were much greater if you were within sight of land.

The Minoan civilization (during the Bronze Age) on the island of Crete in the middle of the eastern Mediterranean Sea, thrived on extensive trade with other nations like Greece, Syria, Egypt, Spain, and Mesopotamia. This required Minoan sailors to spend days and sometimes even weeks out of sight of land. Records from

What was the name of the Viking who discovered Newfoundland and who was his famous father?

KON-TIKI

In 1947, Thor Heyerdahl and five other adventurers set off to cross the Pacific Ocean from east to west on a raft that was a copy of a prehistoric South American vessel. Heyerdahl was attempting to prove that Polynesia could have been settled by people sailing from South America. After an amazing journey of 101 days and 4,300 nautical miles on a raft made from balsa wood, Heyerdahl spotted land. Kon-Tiki and her crew landed on the island of Raroia. This successful voyage proved that the Polynesian islands were within range of prehistoric South American people.

The Kon-Tiki.

A replica of the Kon-Tiki raft will sail the Pacific in 2005 and a grandson of Heyerdahl will be on board.

the Phoenicians, the ancient Israelites, Egyptians, Maltans, Romans, and Greeks all show they had trading partners far away from their home ports.

Leif the Lucky, son of Eric the Red who discovered and named Greenland, came upon Newfoundland around 1000 CE and briefly established a colony in what he called Vineland. The Icelandic sagas, stories passed down from generation to generation, tell the story of how Vikings sailed from Norway to Iceland, then to Greenland, then on to Newfoundland. How did they do it before they had access to the magnetic compass? Unlike the ancient mariners of the Mediterranean, there isn't even evidence that the Vikings had anything that kept time, like an hourglass or sandglass.

Archaeologists have suggested that the Vikings may have used a crystal, like calcite, for orientation. If you hold a piece of calcite up to the sun and look through it, the light is polarized and the crystal turns a different color. Viking sailors might have been able to use the crystal to help figure out where the sun was when obscured by clouds. Sun stones are mentioned in the Icelandic sagas—but there is no real evidence that sun stones were used for navigation.

What are some of the ways ancient Vikings navigated without instruments?

We do know that the Vikings had many ways to determine direction: they knew which direction the winds blew, they had a good idea what it meant when they saw particular birds, and they knew where whales were likely to be at particular times of the year.

Some of the most amazing navigators in the world prior to the development of the magnetic compass were the people of Oceania (another name for the islands in the Central and South Pacific Ocean). Long before Columbus and Magellan and the European age of exploration, a nation of seafarers had already discovered and colonized the vast expanse of Pacific Islands. Some 6,000 years ago, seafarers left islands in eastern Indonesia and the Philippines to branch into the western Pacific. Archaeologists trace their migrations by the cultural materials they brought with them. Shell hooks, coral files, and bone tattooing needles have been found in sites from the Bismark Archipelago, near New Guinea, all the way to the Solomon Islands, Vanuatu, Fiji, Tonga, and Samoa. Scientists call these early seafarers the Lapita people. Adzes and other cutting tools, chipped from obsidian, or volcanic glass, have been found in the ruins of their settlements. Obsidian was evidently one commodity in an extensive network of trade that connected the islands of the Lapita peoples until the dispersal of the culture in 500 BCE. Normally we

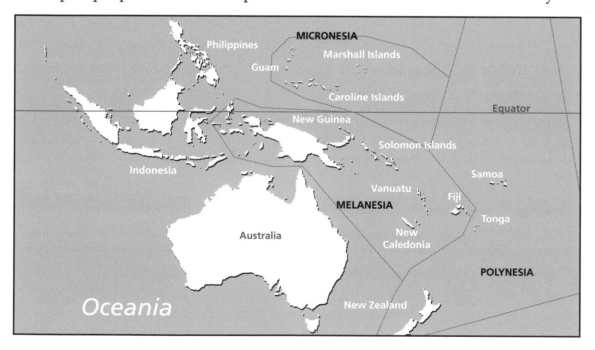

Present-day depiction of an early Lapita navigator.

think of the Europeans as the great explorers of the world, "discovering" the Americas and venturing far and wide across the Pacific all the way to Asia. But when the Greeks were still making short hops between islands in the Aegean, Lapita navigators were making long, open-sea passages without charts, compasses, or instruments. That would be like you traveling across the country without a map.

Over time, as the Lapita people colonized more islands, these settlers developed a unique set of languages and cultural traits, which today distinguish Micronesia from Polynesia and Melanesia, the two other cultural areas of Oceania.

On Tonga and Samoa, the Lapita people developed a distinct Polynesian language and culture. Then about 2,000 years ago they voyaged into the eastern Pacific, making the 1,800-mile windward passage to the Marquesas Islands. Later, perhaps following the migratory flight paths of birds, they discovered and colonized Tahiti, Hawaii, New Zealand, and tiny Easter Island, a feat of seafaring as great as any discovery by a European explorer. Thus, all of Oceania, an area nearly a quarter of the earth, was populated by a single race. Navigators using just the stars, the ocean swells, and the flight paths of birds were making epic ocean voyages in sailing canoes at a time when most Europeans were content to stay in the safety of their villages.

Upon discovering the Hawaiian Islands in 1778, which he named the Sandwich Islands after the Earl of Sandwich, Captain James Cook wrote:

WORDS TO KNOW

Polynesia: *from the Greek poly=many and nesos=island. Over 1,000 islands; a triangle with its three corners at Hawaii, New Zealand, and Easter Island. It covers the central and southern Pacific Ocean.*

Micronesia: *from the Greek micro=small and nesos=island. Islands in the western Pacific bordered by the Philippines to the west, Indonesia to the southwest, and Polynesia to the east.*

Melanesia: *from the Greek mela=black and nesos=island. The oldest of the Pacific people, includes Fiji, New Guinea, Caledonia, Solomon Islands, Vanuatu, Maluku, Torres Strait Islands.*

What are the three basic requirements for successful navigation at sea?

Page 3 Gossip: Earl of Sandwich Insists New Discovery Named for Him

The **Ancient Inquirer**
some time in the year 1778

Cook Discovers Sandwich Islands
Debate Rages Over Origin of Islands' Names

Lorem ipsum dolor sit amet, conse ctetuer adipiscing elit, sed diam no nummy nibh euismod tincidunt ut la oreet dolore magna aliquam erat vo lutpat. Ut wisi enim ad minim venia m, quis nostrud exerci tation ullamc orper suscipit lobortis nisl ut aliquip ex ea commodo consequat. Duis

(Artist Rendition)

"How shall we account for this Nation spreading itself over this Vast ocean? We find them from New Zealand to the South, to these islands to the North and from Easter Island to the Hebrides." Cook had discovered the Polynesians, descendants of the Lapita. The indigenous navigating tradition was still very much alive in Oceania but in the following years of European exploration and trade, these navigators all but disappeared. Now, throughout Polynesia and in much of Micronesia, the tradition is forgotten. The central Caroline Islands is one of the few places where traditional navigation is still practiced and the "talk of the sea" has been passed from father to son in a tradition that stretches back thousands of years.

Mysterious carved statues that dominate Easter Island.

What is the difference between the traditions of Micronesian navigation and European oceanic navigation? There are three basic requirements for a successful navigation system at sea. First, the navigator needs to figure out how he's going to get to his destination by plotting a course. Then he has to maintain that course at sea. And finally, he has to figure out how to measure and compensate for his boat being blown off course by currents, winds, or storms.

European Navigation

Historically, European ocean navigation was a system that integrated charts and instruments. The chart gave European or western navigators the means to find their course by clearly identifying the chosen

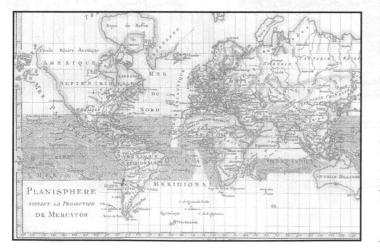

Map of the known world in 1780.

destination. A nautical chart is much like a road map. Islands, reefs, and continents are laid out in correct relation to one another, and on more modern charts, according to Mercator's projection (you'll learn about this later). A compass rose is printed on the chart with geographic north oriented toward the top and lines of latitude and

SOUNDING LINE

Probably the earliest navigator's instrument invented was the sounding line. This is a long line with knots marking distance (the knots marked fathoms, which is a unit for measuring the depth of water and is equal to 1.8 meters or 2 yards). A lead weight was at the end of the line, helping it to sink to the bottom. By counting the number of knots from the water to the sea floor the navigator could determine the depth of the sea. The bottom of the lead weight often had tallow (rendered pig's fat that was used in candle making) rubbed on it so that when the sounding line was brought up, whatever was on the sea floor stuck to the tallow, allowing the sailor to check what kind of sediment lay at the bottom.

As a ship approached the shore, a sailor took frequent soundings. Eventually, this kind of information was added to charts and portolans, *which were maps that showed the coastlines. Portolans started to carry notations indicating what a sailor could expect to find on the ocean floor at any particular depth. If you look at a really old map you might notice words like fine sediment, sand, silt, or smooth round pebbles written at particular depths along the coastline. That way, if a sailor took a sounding and his sounding line brought up sediment that matched a description, it could help determine exactly where the ship was on the map.*

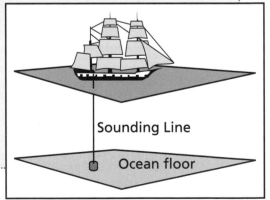

Sounding Line

Ocean floor

WORDS TO KNOW

portolan: *ancient pilot books containing hand-drawn charts and descriptions of harbors and sea coasts.*

lore: *knowledge gained through tradition, passed down from one generation to the next.*

What are the units for measuring the depth of water?

longitude measuring degrees and minutes are drawn onto the chart (one minute equals one nautical mile and 60 minutes equals one degree). With instruments like the compass and sextant, western navigators could check the speed and direction of the currents, keep their course at sea, and fix their position using the sun, moon, stars, and planets. All of these measurements allowed them to produce a dead reckoning, which was regularly updated to keep the ship on course.

Palu, the Micronesian Navigator

The Micronesian system of navigation is called *Etak* and is mastered by *palu*, the navigator. Like European navigation, Micronesian navigation is an integrated system. But unlike a European or western navigation system it does not rely on written materials and instruments. Rather, it combines a vast body of lore and the navigator's own senses. The palu guides his outrigger canoe by the stars at night and with his knowledge of ocean swells and currents during the day and on overcast nights. He keeps the star paths (the rising and setting of the stars) of 32 stars, which form a kind of star compass, in his head at all times. He knows which stars are over which islands during any particular season and time of night. He also recognizes eight "waves," one from each octant (one-eighth) of the compass. Etak assumes that palu, the navigator, is in a canoe that is stationary, and that the islands move on the sea around him. This concept is hard for us to even imagine because we are sure that the canoe is moving. But with the same conviction, the palu is certain that his canoe is stationary and the world is moving around him. In his worldview, islands come toward him and move away from him.

The palu must be able to read the stars, the waves, and the clouds, as well as the creatures of the sea. He knows which birds inhabit which islands and he also has been taught that each island has a ring of specific sea creatures around it. When he sets out in his outrigger sailing canoe, it is with this knowledge in his head. Nothing is written down. And all these strands of knowledge interconnect in the palu's mind and allow him to successfully guide his canoe.

The palu is responsible for guiding his people to food and to other islands and because of this knowledge, he holds a revered status in his culture, much like a chief. If he cannot guide the fishermen to the fish, his people starve. His knowledge of the sea and of the world was taught to him by his father and he alone can pass this knowledge—the "talk of the sea"—on to the next generation.

The Silk Road

Not all navigation occurs on water. People also had to make their way across unknown expanses of land. They found themselves braving the elements—fighting windstorms in a desert or howling snowstorms on mountain passes—in their quest to discover new lands to settle or new people to trade with. One of the most famous overland routes was a trade route known as the Silk Road. When you hear the phrase "Silk Road," don't think of a single highway stretching from southern China to the Mediterranean Sea, rather, think of interconnected roads and trails weaving their way from east to west, bringing new ideas and merchandise to all the towns and villages along the way. These routes connected far-off and distant cultures that had arisen in the Mediterranean, India, and the Far East.

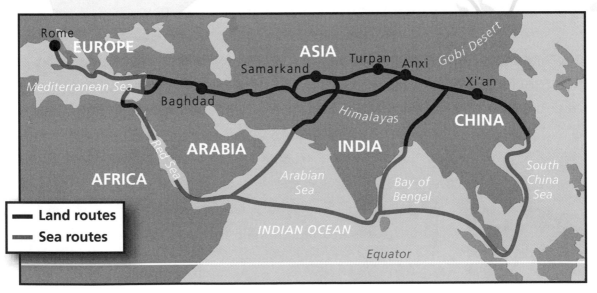

This important trade route had its beginnings over 2,000 years ago when a Chinese emperor sent an emissary to the west in search of better horses. Within a couple of decades, the Romans saw their first pieces of silk fabric from China and wanted more. Pliny, a famous Roman intellectual, opined that silk was from trees and was "obtained by removing the down from the leaves with the help of water." The silk merchants of China knew they had a valuable commodity and for hundreds of years tried to keep the details of silk production (sericulture) a secret. Everyone was searched at the borders of silk-producing towns in China, but it was inevitable that the secret would eventually be revealed. One story tells of a princess who was betrothed to a prince in a far-off western region and how she smuggled silkworm eggs in her hair and mulberry seeds in her medicines (silkworms eat mulberry leaves).

Silkworm.

daavestravelcorner.com

Spices for trade.

The Silk Road also introduced Europe and the West to spices—particularly nutmeg, cloves, and peppercorns—from the East. These spices only grew on particular islands in the Far East known as the Spice Islands. As Arab traders pushed further east and Eastern traders pushed west, they began to exchange goods, including spices, which became worth more than their weight in gold. It was said that every time a load of spices changed hands, the price went up a hundred-fold. And sometimes spices traded hands about a hundred times in the course of their journey from east to west.

WORDS TO KNOW

Far East: *China, Japan, and other countries of East Asia.*

emissary: *someone sent on a mission.*

sericulture: *the production of raw silk by raising silkworms.*

Spice Islands: *the Maluku Islands, now part of Indonesia. Until the late 1700s, the only source of cloves, nutmeg, and mace.*

BACTRIAN CAMELS

Bactrian camels (Camelus bactrianus) are the ancestors of all domestic camels. They were formerly found in the deserts of Mongolia and northwestern China and into Kazahkstan but are currently only found in a few isolated places. These two-humped camels are extremely well adapted to harsh desert climates—they have dense eyelashes and narrow nostrils that close tightly during sandstorms. Their two-toed feet have connective tissue between the toes that allows their feet to spread to make it easier to walk on the sand. They eat mainly shrubs and their humps store excess fat, allowing them to go for many days without food. They can also go for a period of time without water (it is not stored in the humps) because their bodies are good at conserving water. When they locate water, they're able to drink up to 57 liters at one time. Some of these camels have developed the ability to drink salt water— and they're the only mammals capable of this feat.

Most merchants or traders had several routes to choose from when traveling along the Silk Road. Often, the shortest routes were the most dangerous because of treacherous conditions—too hot in the summer, too cold in the winter, or swarming with bandits—so traders had to balance speed with safety. Routes were established based on geography and climate, to minimize the amount of time in the mountains or in the deserts. Towns or oases (places where caravans stopped to rest and get food and water) sprung up along these routes. Many traders traveled together in caravans of up to 100 camels or more and then hired guards to patrol the route for bandits. Traders used Bactrian camels, or the camels with two humps, which had amazing endurance for the long, hard trip and could be loaded with up to 500 pounds of merchandise.

WORDS TO KNOW

Dark Ages: *the period in European history between the fall of the Roman Empire and the Middle Ages, 500–1100 CE.*

Statue of Buddha.

A merchant would bring his goods to a market in a trading town and then sell or trade them before continuing on his journey. Most traders never traveled the entire length of the Silk Road because they traded their merchandise along the way and once it was sold or traded there was no reason to continue on.

The height of trade on the Silk Road occurred during the Tang Dynasty (618–907 CE) in China. The Chinese sent silk, furs, spices, jade, bronze, iron, and lacquer objects west in exchange for gold, gems, ivory, glass, perfumes, and textiles. There was a constant flow of ideas and customs along the trade route as well. Buddhism—which would become an extremely important religion in China—made its way from India to China via a Silk Road route. The Silk Road trade route experienced a sharp decline in the tenth century as Europe entered into a period known as the Dark Ages. The Second Crusades in the thirteenth century—a time when European armies tried to spread Christendom into lands held by non-Christians—created a new demand for Asian goods in Europe. Why? Because when the Crusaders returned home they brought goods from the East—like silk and spices—back with them.

Navigating the well-traveled routes along the Silk Road was easy. While the geography changed dramatically from rolling plains to almost impassable mountains to impenetrable deserts, the stars in the sky remained the same for travelers on this predominantly east-

The Crusades.

MARCO POLO (1254–1324)

A lot of what we know about the Far East and the Silk Road comes from the travels of Marco Polo. This amazing, intrepid traveler was born in thirteenth-century Venice, a powerful trading city in Italy. Marco's father and uncle were among the first European traders to make their way east all the way to China along the Silk Road. When they came back home to Venice, part of their mission was to obtain certain items like letters and some oil from the lamp at the Holy Sepulchre from the Pope in Rome. These items had been requested by Kublai Khan, the Mongol ruler of what was the largest empire in the world, which included China. When they set out for the Far East again, they took along 17-year-old Marco.

Marco Polo traveled throughout Asia for the next 24 years. He became a great friend and advisor to Kublai Khan. He served in his court and was sent on missions to Burma, India, and throughout China. A gifted linguist, he mastered four languages, which helped in his service to the Khan.

We know a great deal about Marco Polo's travels even though they happened over 700 years ago because they were recorded in a book. Within a year of returning to Venice, Marco Polo found himself in prison in Genoa after being captured by the Genoans during a sea battle. (Venice and Genoa were fierce rival Italian city-states and were always competing for control of the Silk Road trade before the goods entered Europe.)

While in prison, Marco Polo dictated stories of his travels to a fellow inmate, Rustichello of Pisa. The story of his travels was known in his time as **The Description of the World** *or* **The Travels of Marco Polo.** *His account of*

Why was the Bactrian Camel so important to trade on the Silk Road?

the wealth of Cathay (China), the might of the Mongol empire, and the exotic customs of India and Africa made his book an immediate bestseller. Later it became one of the most popular books in medieval Europe and its impact on contemporary Europe was tremendous. The book was affectionately known as **Il Milione, the Million Lies,** *and Marco Polo earned the nickname of Marco Milione because few people believed that his stories could be true.*

What can we learn about navigation from Marco Polo? Well, even though people during his time didn't believe a lot of what he claimed, some of the mapmakers of the day incorporated his information into important maps of the later Middle Ages. These maps, like the Catalan World Map of 1375, were studied with great interest by explorers like Henry the Navigator (a Portuguese prince who organized and encouraged exploration) and Christopher Columbus.

As more people try to trace or recreate Marco Polo's routes as outlined in his book, they're finding that the information, even though 700 years old, is still accurate today. His system of measuring distances by days' journey has turned out to be remarkably accurate. In the 1960s, writer Tim Severin tried to trace one of Marco Polo's routes to China by hopping on a motorcycle in Venice and heading east with only **Marco Polo's Travels** *as his guidebook. While traveling through villages and towns in Iran, Iraq, and Afghanistan, he was able to pinpoint his modern-day position by reading Polo's ancient descriptions.*

west route. The main trade routes lay between 30 and 40 degrees latitude in the Northern Hemisphere. Knowledge of the stars within this portion of the sky moved along the Silk Road with the more tangible commodities. In addition to trading tangible goods, the Silk Road was a bit like today's Internet, a place where information and ideas were exchanged over thousands of miles. Where would

WORDS TO KNOW

intrepid: *not afraid or intimidated.*

we be today without the plow, gunpowder, paper, or movable type—all inventions from the East that came overland via the Silk Road?

Old map of Spice Islands.

The end of trade along the Silk Road came in the fifteenth century. The Ming Dynasty (1368–1644 CE) of China closed its borders because of what it saw as corrupting influences from the West. Around the same time, Europeans discovered a reliable sea route to Asia, which proved to be less dangerous, less costly, and less time-consuming than traveling by land. Once Europeans discovered the Spice Islands by sea they were no longer dependent on Arab traders from the East for spies. Persians and Italians had also discovered how to manufacture silk, which lessened the Western demand for silk from the East.

. . . silk, furs, spices, jade, bronze, iron, and lacquer objects . . . in exchange for gold, gems, ivory, glass, perfumes, dyes, and textiles.

THE WORLD EXPANDS
THE AGE OF EUROPEAN EXPLORATION

Although it seems like a cliché, the magnetic compass really is the instrument that changed how we view the world. It allowed explorers to push far into the unknown world and make it the known world, opening up maritime trade routes that we benefit from to this day.

The Compass

How and why does a compass work? The earth's core is molten iron that swirls around in a spherical pattern. This sets up a dynamo action resulting in magnetism, a gigantic magnetic field surrounding the earth where invisible lines of force exist that run between two points called a magnetic north and a magnetic south pole. The magnetic field "pulls" on iron

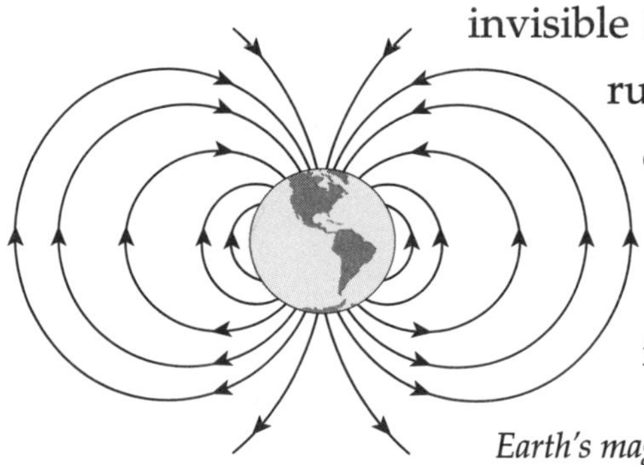

Earth's magnetic field.

Learn about latitude and longitude

Explore early maps

Make your own compass

Meet the great explorers and circumnavigate the globe

Measure your local time

MAGNETIC NORTH VS GEOGRAPHIC NORTH

The magnetic north pole is not the same as the geographic North Pole, which puts a wrinkle in determining an accurate bearing. This is called magnetic deviation (the magnet deviates from geographic north) and scientific charts and tables were drawn up showing how deviation changes from place to place, and from time to time. This allowed a navigator to "correct" for deviation and produce bearings and readings that corresponded to geographic north. Today, magnetic north lies about 1,000 miles south of geographic north, in the vicinity of Prince of Wales Island in Canada. If you are trying to plot a compass course on a map in Maine, you would have to set your compass or correct for a declination of about 20 degrees.

and similar metals and either attracts or repels other magnets depending on their orientation. Like poles (north-north or south-south) repel each other and unlike poles (north-south) attract.

The compass needle is a tiny magnet suspended in air or liquid so it can rotate freely and orient itself. Because the needle is magnetized, it will always seek to be oriented with the earth's magnetic field. Over time, mariners realized that a compass needle can be affected by metal objects on a ship so they learned how to correct this problem.

The origins of the compass are mysterious, but most certainly lie in ancient China. The Chinese recognized the magnetic properties of lodestone (a naturally occurring magnetized form of the mineral magnetite). The palace gate of Ch'in Shi Huang-ti, who ruled China until 210 BCE, was made from lodestone and anyone who tried to enter the palace carrying concealed iron weapons was detected. You can think of this as the first metal detector.

Ancient Chinese texts refer to ladles or spoons with the mysterious quality that they always pointed south (which means the other end pointed north). These ladles were made of lodestone and functioned as compasses. Chinese emperors viewed south as the imperial direction.

By 1040 CE the Chinese were constructing and using iron-fish compasses. They made a fish—thin as a leaf—out of iron by pouring molten iron into a mold and letting it cool and solidify in the direction of the earth's magnetic field. This creates magnetism in the metal in a process called thermoremanence. This thin iron fish would then be floated in a dish of water and the fish's head would naturally point south, in the imperial direction. What's interesting is that there's scant evidence that the Chinese used the magnetic compass for navigating. Rather, they used the compass in feng shui, which is the practice of placing buildings—and windows, doors, and furniture within buildings—in certain orientations, in belief that properly placed objects would help ensure that life would be in harmony.

SOUTH

The magnetic compass was first mentioned in the West in the writings of Alexander Neckam (1157–1217), an English Augustinian monk. In his book *De Naturis Rerum* (1187), he writes:

> The sailors, moreover, as they sail over the sea, when in cloudy weather they can no longer profit by the light of the sun, or when the world is wrapped up in the darkness of the shades of night, and they are ignorant to what point of the compass their ship's course is directed, they touch the magnet with a needle. This then whirls round in a circle until, when its motion ceases, its point looks direct to the north.

WORDS TO KNOW

bearing: *a direction or a path.*

magnetic deviation: *the error of a compass due to local magnetic disturbances.*

declination: *comparable to latitude, measured in degrees north of the equator.*

lodestone: *the mineral magnetite, which has magnetic properties.*

thermoremanence: *letting molten iron cool in the direction of the earth's magnetic field so the iron becomes magnetized.*

ACTIVITY

Make Your Own Compass

In this activity we learn how to make our own compass. It won't be as accurate as something you can buy from the store, but it will give you a really good idea how and why a compass works.

Supplies:

- Half gallon paper milk carton
- 1.5 inch nail with a head (steel, not iron)
- Cardboard
- Large metal paperclip
- A magnet
- Glue or tape
- Paper
- Markers

2 inches

Instructions:

- Cut the top off the milk carton so you have an open "box" with sides about two inches high.
- Poke the nail up through the center of the bottom of the milk carton so the point of the nail is sticking up in the center of the box.

2 inches

- Cut a circle out of the cardboard, making sure that it fits in the box. Be careful to cut a good circle—perhaps trace around a jar lid.
- Straighten out the metal paperclip and lay it across the center of the cardboard circle. If it is longer than the circle, cut to fit. (Hint: Make sure it's a large paperclip because a small one is too light-weight for this compass.)

Where is magnetic north? How many miles from the North Pole?

- Magnetize the paperclip by running the magnet back and forth across the entire paperclip for several minutes. Test the paperclip to see if it's magnetized by placing it against something metal.

- Glue or tape the paperclip to the cardboard circle so that it lies just slightly off-center.

- Place your cardboard circle on top of a piece of paper and trace it.

- Cut out the paper circle.

- Create a compass rose on the paper circle making sure you notate N, NE, E, SE, S, SW, W, and NW.

- Glue the paper circle onto the cardboard circle so that the paperclip is sandwiched between the two. MAKE SURE THAT ONE END OF YOUR PAPERCLIP IS UNDER NORTH AND THE OTHER IS UNDER SOUTH.

- Place the center of the bottom of your cardboard circle on the point of the nail. Don't poke the nail all the way through but make a good indent so the cardboard circle is resting comfortably on the nail but can still turn.

- Slowly turn your compass box and watch how the compass rose continues to point to north.

When was the compass invented?

Some put the invention of the magnetic compass in the West in the Mediterranean port town of Amalfi. From the twelfth century through the mid-fourteenth century, Amalfi was the major naval power on the Mediterranean. Whoever controlled the Mediterranean Sea, controlled the trade. While the compass was not actually invented in Amalfi, it was probably perfected there. About this time, the compass was transformed from a needle (or thin fish) floating in water to the compass we know today: a round box containing a compass card with the wind rose calibrated into 360 degrees and a magnetic element (a needle).

The magnetic compass became standard equipment on ships sometime in the fourteenth century. This was invaluable for sailing out at sea, like in the Mediterranean and the Atlantic, whose depths precluded effective use of the sounding line. Navigators could now use charts and maps that included a combination of sounding information (the depth of the water and materials on the sea floor) and bearing (sailing by a set course). The Portuguese and Spanish took navigation to the next level by using celestial observations in combination with a compass and an astrolabe (an early form of the sextant) to estimate positions. Christopher Columbus was a whiz at dead reckoning—estimating position by figuring out speed and time traveled, and extending the result along the compass course from the previous known position.

Once the compass was applied to navigation, the whole world opened up. It's hard to imagine that an object that will fit in your hand could have such an enormous impact, but this navigational aid allowed travelers to go across great expanses of uncharted territory with the confidence that they could return again.

WORDS TO KNOW

celestial: *relating to the stars.*
astrolabe: *an instrument used to calculate latitude.*
cardinal points: *north, south, east, and west.*

Maps: Navigating on Land and Sea

What do we want to learn from a map? How about where things are in relation to one another? Or the scale, so we can know how far it is from this point of the stream to that distant mountain or measure the width of the mouth of that bay. This knowledge will help determine how long it's going to take to travel these distances. A good map will give you orientation (in other words, tell you which direction is north), a scale (an inch equals so many miles), and will show basic landmarks. The more detailed a map, the easier it is to figure out where you are.

The earliest maps we have come from Iraq and date to about 2,300 BCE. These maps, inscribed on clay tablets, show settlements, streams, mountains, and some scale. They also show three of the four cardinal points (north, east, and west) by naming the winds associated with them. The south wind is missing. Ancient maps were oriented east, presumably because that was the direction of sunrise. Medieval Christian maps were also oriented east because that was supposed to be the direction of Paradise.

Ptolemy.

One of the most influential early mapmakers was Ptolemy, who lived in Alexandria, Egypt in the first century CE. He wrote two influential books—one on astronomy (*Almagest*) and the other on geography (*Geography*)—and his influence on how we view the world persists to this day.

What's neat is that 2,000 years ago, Ptolemy came up with a definition for geography that we still use today. "Geography," he wrote, "is a representation in pictures of the whole known world together with the phenomena which are contained therein." What this means in practical terms is that you don't put things on a map you haven't actually seen. Exploration and discovery always have to precede cartography (mapmaking).

Ptolemy thought the earth was round and when making his map of the known world, he worked with lines of latitude and longitude. In mapmaking these are known as parallels (east-west) and meridians (north-south).

Who was a whiz at estimating his positions at sea using a compass?

LAND MILES VS. NAUTICAL MILES

While we're looking at definitions let's look at the difference between a mile on land and a nautical mile. The mile was originally a Roman measure of 1,000 paces, which equaled about 1,618 yards. Along Roman roads, they used to erect stones every mile (milestones) to measure the distance from Rome. Today, a land mile is 1,760 yards, or 5,280 feet because in 1593, Queen Elizabeth I of England proclaimed it to be so (that's why it's known as a "statute" mile). But you can't measure the ocean by paces. So using geometry, a nautical mile is based on the length of one minute of arc, which is ¹⁄₆₀ of a degree. Here's how it works. There are 360 degrees in a circle. If you measure the circumference of the earth at 0 degrees latitude (or the equator) in feet and then divide that number by 360 degrees and then divide that number by 60 minutes (for 60 minutes in each degree), you come up with the number of feet in a nautical mile.

So at the equator there are 60 nautical miles to each degree.

As you move north or south, the circumference of the earth becomes smaller and smaller so the number of miles in each degree gets less. The mile finally had to be defined as a standardized number so the British assigned it a standard average value of 6,080 feet. This makes a nautical mile 800 feet longer than a land mile. It's too bad we don't use the same "mile" on both land and sea.

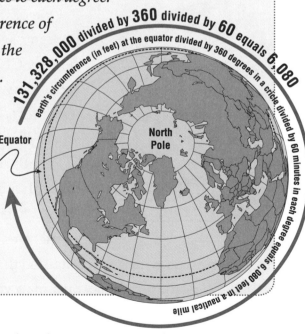

131,328,000 divided by 360 divided by 60 equals 6,080

earth's circumference (in feet) at the equator divided by 360 degrees in a circle divided by 60 minutes in each degree equals 6,080 feet in a nautical mile

0° latitude—Equator

North Pole

WORDS TO KNOW:

summer solstice: *in the Northern Hemisphere, when the sun is at its northernmost point, on June 21.*

Tropic of Cancer: *the northernmost latitude where the sun can shine directly overhead on the summer solstice, at latitude 23°30′N.*

DETERMINING THE CIRCUMFERENCE OF THE EARTH

Eratosthenes (c. 276–194 BCE) was born in Cyrene on the north coast of Africa, educated in Athens, and came to Egypt in his thirties. He was a skilled geographer, astronomer, poet, and literary critic and served as a librarian at the famous library of Alexandria. He solved many mathematical problems but his greatest feat was to measure the size of the earth.

He placed a pole perfectly upright in the ground to make a simple sundial. At noon in Alexandria on the summer solstice *he measured the length of the shadow, and calculated that the sun was 7 degrees south of the vertical. He then traveled south to Aswan on the* Tropic of Cancer. *Two thousand years ago it was known by its Greek name, Syene, and possessed a number of deep wells.*

Eratosthenes had heard that if you looked into one of the wells at Syene at noon on the summer solstice you could see the sun reflected in the water at the bottom. Because the water surface was horizontal, he realized this must mean the sun was exactly overhead. However, a ray of sunlight falling on Alexandria at noon on midsummer's day was at an angle of 7 degrees. Consequently the difference in angle of the sun between the two places was one fifty-first of a full circle (360/7 = 51), and therefore the distance between Syene and Alexandria was exactly one fifty-first part of the circumference of the earth.

Therefore, if he could measure the distance between the two cities, he could estimate the size of the earth. Luckily he had the use of the Royal Pacers: soldiers trained to pace precisely the same distance in each stride. Counting their strides, he was able to measure the distance between the two cities, approximately 500 miles. As a result he calculated that the circumference of the earth was 51 multiplied by 500, or 25,500 miles. This figure was accurate to within about one percent of the true figure, which is about 24,901 miles. While Syene was not quite on the Tropic of Cancer and the distance between Syene and Alexandria was a bit less than 500 miles, Eratosthenes was remarkably close nonetheless.

He figured out that parallels, or lines of latitude, had to be parallel to one another, whereas meridians had to be arcs of a circle that came together at the poles. He knew that when he drew a map of the world on a flat surface there had to be certain adjustments to retain a semblance of spherical properties with a minimum of distortion. Ptolemy's map projection comes closest to being what is now known as an equal-area projection: where equal areas on the earth's surface appear as equal areas on the map.

Another innovation by Ptolemy was to orient the map with north at the top and east to the right (that's the way we read maps today), his reason being that much more was known about the northern latitudes.

Ptolemy's ideas were pretty much lost to the Western world for more than a thousand years after much of the city of Alexandria was destroyed in 391 CE. The library that housed Ptolemy's works was sacked and the contents were burned. It was only through the efforts of some Arab scholars that Ptolemy's works weren't lost forever. Although the originals were burned, copies and works based on the originals were used by Arab scholars as they developed their own cartographic traditions. Ptolemy's ideas were all but forgotten in the West until the Arabic versions were translated back into Greek in the thirteenth century and then into Latin by the early fifteenth century. After Medieval times (also known as the Dark Ages), Europeans were ready for Ptolemy's ideas, which guided some important explorers in their search for a westward sea route to the Far East.

Lines of Latitude

parallels

Road maps developed as early as the Roman Empire. Thought to be used by Roman soldiers and early travelers, these maps

Lines of Longitude

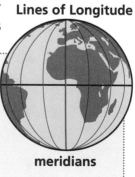

meridians

PARALLELS AND MERIDIANS

Parallels on a map equal the lines of latitude and run east–west. They are parallel to each other. Meridians on a map are lines of longitude, which actually curve toward and meet at the poles. Meridians run north–south.

PTOLEMY'S ERRORS

Ptolemy made three basic errors. First, he put the earth at the center of the universe. We still speak in Ptolemic terms when we say, "the sun rises in the east and sets in the west," which presumes the sun revolves around the earth rather than the other way around. His other error was to reject earlier measurements of the circumference of the earth, which were remarkably accurate. The result was the assumption that the world was about three-fourths its actual size. He also assumed that Asia extended much farther to the east than it does. These last two assumptions led Columbus to think he had reached Asia when he had actually reached the West Indies in the Caribbean Sea in 1492.

show major roads as straight lines with no attempt to show true course or proper scale. But the distances between places were written in, which made the maps very practical.

Old map of the Holy Land.

Early maps of a sort were developed by medieval Christians. These maps are more like guidebooks and give directions and information about places and distances that would be useful for pilgrims traveling between Europe and the Holy Land. The maps included locations of hostels and places for changing horses and donkeys.

Early mariners created sailing books giving sailing instructions based on the directions of the wind rose. By the twelfth century, sailing instructions to every port throughout the entire Mediterranean were available. These directions read like modern sailing directions—they could tell people which direction to follow by letting them know which wind to sail with, and how long they should be on

ACTIVITY

Understanding Latitude

Lines of latitude have different lengths so distances between degrees are different. For instance, at the equator, which is 0 degrees latitude, there are about 70 land miles in one degree (25,000 miles divided by 360 degrees). Just imagine how important it was to understand this information if you were heading out on an ocean exploration. Using the information given on the following chart, determine the distances between the points on each line of latitude. You're given the number of degrees that separates each point. For example, points A–B on latitude 60° = 35 miles x 50 degrees = 1,750 miles.

Latitude	Land Miles in 1 degree
Equator or 0°	70
10°N or S	69
20°N or S	65
30°N or S	60
40°N or S	53
50°N or S	45
60°N or S	35
70°N or S	24
80°N or S	12

90°N—North Pole
80°
70°
60° A 50° B
50°
40° C 89° D
30°
20° E 94° F
10°
0° G 135° equator H
10° I 67° J
20°
30° K 59° L
40°
50° M 125° M
60°
70° O 48° P
80°
90°S—South Pole

the water in order to reach their destination. Sometimes really, really old maps have wonderfully drawn pictures of men's heads with their cheeks puffed out blowing in a particular direction. These were the heads of the figures of the named winds—the same named winds that show up on the wind rose.

Around the turn of the fourteenth century, the first accurate coastal sailing charts—called portolan charts—were developed. These probably began as maps drawn from the written descriptions found in pilot books, which were known as *portolani* in Italian (hence the name portolan). Pilot books were sailing and harbor guides summarizing—in words—the accumulated knowledge of generations of sailors.

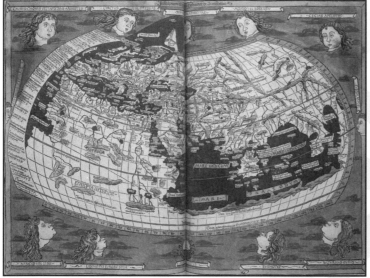

Ptolemy's map showing 12 winds.

Portolans were oriented north and included a wind rose that looked a lot like a compass. A wind rose was divided into eight equal directional points representing the primary wind directions, which corresponded to N, NE, E, SE, S, SW, W, and NW. All sailors knew their winds. With the development of the compass, a network of rhumb lines were added. These lines crisscrossed all major bodies of water and radiated from a number of wind roses spread about the map. A sailor would set his course on one or several of these lines until he reached landfall.

In 1375 the Catalan Atlas, which gathered information from a number of portolans and placed them on six maps, was published. This atlas showed the extent of the known world and combined the detail and accuracy of portolan charts with the latest scientific information. Unlike other portolans, inland towns and rivers were drawn on these atlas maps. For the first time, maps were being drawn to be useful to all travelers.

WORDS TO KNOW

rhumb lines: *constant course lines.*

What is a portolan chart?

The Age of Discovery and the Great Explorers

The mid- to late-fifteenth century was an amazing time for European exploration. Someone once called exploration "planned discovery" and that phrase fits well. Portuguese seamen were sailing to the Atlantic island groups—the Azores, Madeiras, and the Canaries—and then heading down the West African coast. The Portuguese were being sent out by Prince Henry the Navigator, who organized and encouraged expeditions. Prince Henry, who was not a ruler in Portugal because he was a younger son, had the time to pursue his fascination with exploration. He was determined to find a sea route to Asia and the kinds of valuable goods written about by Marco Polo.

Cape of Good Hope

A sea route from Portugal to Asia!

By this point, Ptolemy's *Geography* had been rediscovered by Europeans, which renewed discussion about the circumference of the earth. As the Portuguese seaman made their way down the coast of West Africa, they completed detailed charts. They also included reasonably accurate latitudes on their charts because they knew how to determine latitude using the North Star.

In the latter part of the century, Bartholomew Dias rounded the tip of Africa, thereby discovering the Cape of Good Hope. A decade later, in 1498, Vasco da Gama sailed from the Cape Verde Islands around the Cape of Good Hope and reached the western coast of India. A sea route to Asia had been found! Da Gama was an amazingly good sailor and the charts he made show a high degree of accuracy.

Christopher Columbus (1451–1506)

"In fourteen hundred and ninety-two, Columbus sailed the ocean blue"—who among us doesn't know this rhyme from about the age of four?

When Columbus set sail for Asia

Bahamian stamps depicting discovery by Columbus.

SOME AGE OF EXPLORATION EXPLORERS

1487—Bartholomew Dlus, Portuguese, discovers the southern tip of Africa, the Cape of Good Hope.

1492 — Christopher Columbus, Italian, stumbles upon the West Indies thinking he's reached India.

1497— John Cabot (Giovanni Caboto), Italian, searches for the Northwest Passage, a waterway across North America, and discovers Newfoundland.

1497–1499— Vasco da Gama, Portuguese, discovers an ocean route from Portugal to India.

Christopher Columbus

Ponce de León

1502—Amerigo Vespucci, Italian, returns from explorations in the New World and gets two continents named after him.

1513—Juan Ponce de León, Spanish, searches for the Fountain of Youth in Florida.

1519–1522—Ferdinand Magellan, Portuguese, and his crew sail around the world.

Magellan's route

1534—Jacques Cartier, French, discovers the St. Lawrence River and the Great Lakes.

1539–1542—Hernando de Soto, Spanish, explores the southeastern United States.

1540—Francisco Vásquez de Coronado, Spanish, explores the southwestern United States and his expedition discovers the Grand Canyon.

1577—Sir Francis Drake becomes the first Englishman to sail around the world.

Sir Francis Drake

What European explorer discovered the Grand Canyon?

(which was where he really wanted to go when the West Indies got in the way), he was armed with a whole set of false navigational assumptions. Like Ptolemy, Columbus believed two things that were wrong: first, that the circumference of the earth was much smaller

Rumors of dragons and monsters raise odds against return.

The Inquirer

some time in the year 1492

Columbus Set Sail for Orient

Onlookers Confused—Heading West to Get to the East???

Asia or Bust

Asia or Bust

Lorem ipsum dolor sit amet, consetetuer adipiscing elit, sed diam nonummy nibh euismod tincidunt ut laoreet dolore magna aliquam erat volutpat. Ut wisi enim ad minim veniam, quis nostrud exerci tation ullamcorper suscipit lobortis nisl ut aliquip ex ea commodo consequat. Duis autem vel eum iriure dolor in hendre

(Artist's Rendition)

than it really was, and, second, that the east-west length of Eurasia (the continents of Europe and Asia together) was much larger than it really was. The effect of these two misperceptions was that Columbus believed he had to cover less than 3,000 miles of open ocean in order to reach Asia (when in actuality, Japan lies over 9,000 miles further away—as the crow flies!).

WHO REALLY DISCOVERED AMERICA?

Why is our country named after Amerigo Vespucci, who very few people have ever heard of, rather than Christopher Columbus? Vespucci (1454–1512) was an Italian explorer who was the first person to realize that the Americas were separate from the continent of Asia. He sailed in search of a passage to India in 1499, seven years after Columbus first landed in the West Indies. Vespucci made two voyages between 1499 and 1502 and possibly a third one in 1503.

But the big breakthrough came on Vespucci's second trip. This was the realization that what he was looking at was not India at all, but an entirely new continent. He verified this by following the coast of South America to within 400 miles of Tierra del Fuego. Columbus found the New World, but Vespucci was the one who recognized that it was a new world.

For many years, controversy surrounded Vespucci. Many people thought he was a fraud who never made the trips he claimed to have made. There were no journals, logs, or maps of the journeys, but he did write two letters that have survived.

Amerigo Vespucci

He compounded his problems by underestimating the distance of a degree of longitude at the equator. As a result, he further underestimated the distance he would need to sail on his planned course at 28 degrees latitude. (Remember that the lines of longitude curve toward each other as they get further away from 0 degrees latitude—the equator).

Coincidentally, the calculations Columbus made to determine the distance to Asia were pretty close to the distance he actually covered when he reached the West Indies, making the mistaken belief that he had reached Asia quite believable after all.

The West Indies and the Caribbean Sea.

What's amazing is that Columbus had the nerve to sail off into the unknown in the first place. Mariners up to that point were very accustomed to sailing with portolans, which were detailed maps of the coasts. There was a great fear of the unknown—for example, there were some who thought dragons and sea monsters lived beyond the horizon—and portolans provided a kind of security by presenting the known world. Columbus sailed west based on a theory that he would find landfall at a particular place and distance. Even though his theory was based on false assumptions, it was a great leap for him, in particular, and for oceanic exploration in general when he set sail and eventually landed in the New World.

Meanwhile, at about the same time that Columbus set sail and landed in the New World, Spanish and Portuguese mariners began exploring the coast of South America. Amerigo Vespucci completed three voyages that reconnoitered the coast of Brazil. Vespucci was immortalized on a map made in 1507 that depicted the coastline from Newfoundland to Argentina and had the word "America" written across Brazil. By the mid-sixteenth century, maps were showing both North and South America.

Who was America named after?

ASTROLABE

The astrolabe was invented by the Greeks and was used up through the Middle Ages to determine latitude. An astrolabe measured the angle, or the altitude, between the zenith (the point directly overhead) and a celestial body (like the North Star). A disc was calibrated, or marked off, in degrees, and a movable arm was attached at the center of the disc. Christopher Columbus used an astrolabe, as did Ferdinand Magellan, when they were on their historic voyages. Arab travelers used astrolabes to navigate in the desert, which was like an ocean of sand with no visible landmarks.

An inherent problem with using an astrolabe was determining the zenith—there was no star marking the point directly overhead. Also, astrolabes were difficult to use on a rolling, pitching ship, but when they were taken ashore, they were invaluable in determining approximate latitude.

Ferdinand Magellan (1480–1521)

In 1519, Magellan set off in search of a western route to Asia. He had studied all available maps and had determined that it might be possible to sail around South America. What he didn't know was how unbelievably large the Pacific Ocean was going to be. Like Columbus, he believed Ptolemy's numbers about the circumference of the earth, which grossly underestimated the distance he was going to have to travel.

He did discover the strait that today bears his name— the Strait of Magellan—as he made his way around the southern end of South America. This is perhaps the most treacherous stretch of water in the world. As ocean currents come down both the east and west coasts of South America, they converge and create a seething cauldron of waves, howling winds, and fierce weather. The eastern entrance of the strait is calm but

soon the water gets funneled through a channel that separates mainland South America from the large island of Tierra del Fuego (named "land of fire" by Magellan because as they passed through the strait, they were amazed by the fires the native people lit on the shores and the surrounding hills).

As he headed out of the strait, Magellan faced the vast Pacific Ocean where he managed to miss most of the island chains before reaching Guam four months later. Magellan guided his ships by compass and celestial navigation alone, setting his bearing and then staying remarkably true to course. The intrepid navigator finally reached the Philippines where he was killed while trying to mediate a skirmish between two warring native groups.

Magellan's expedition made its way home via the Indian Ocean and the Cape of Good Hope. Out of five ships that initially set sail, only one made

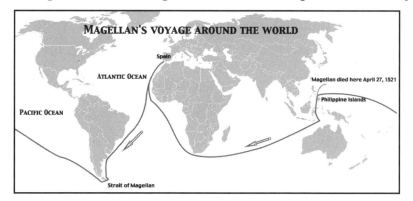

it home and only 35 of the original 280 men survived the three-year voyage.

This historic voyage—the first circumnavigation of the earth—proved that the earth was round and could be sailed around. This had a tremendous and immediate impact on mapmaking. As new lands were discovered and explored, maps were updated to represent the new knowledge about the earth.

Gerardus Mercator (1512–1594)

A gifted mapmaker born in Flanders (now Belgium), Mercator spent his life recording the great discoveries of the sixteenth century. He was determined to

ACTIVITY

Make a Simple Astrolabe

An astrolabe helped explorers find their latitude by measuring angles using the stars as reference points.

Supplies:

- Thread, protractor, paper clip, and tape
- Long straw or paper rolled into a ¼-inch tube
- Small notebook and pencil

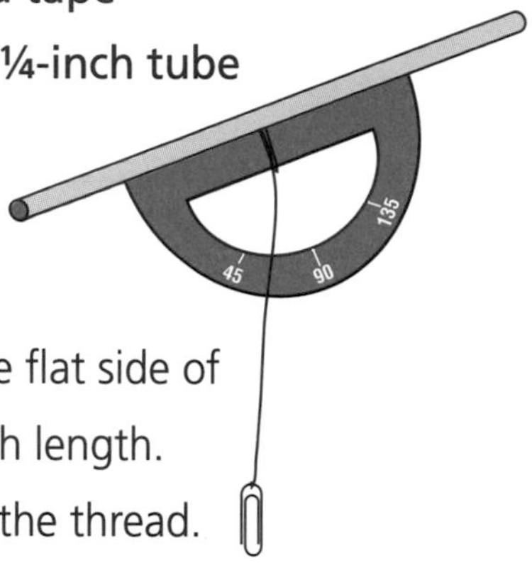

Instructions:

- Tie a thread around the middle of the flat side of the protractor leaving about an 8-inch length.
- Tie the paper clip to the long end of the thread.
- Tape the flat edge of the protractor to the length of the straw.
- Go outside at night when there are lots of stars out.
- Identify the North Star (see page 10).
- Look at the North Star through your straw, making sure the thread with the paperclip weight is hanging free.
- Hold the thread in place against the protractor after you locate the North Star.
- Take it down from your eye and read the degrees on the protractor where the thread crosses. (Read the inner set of numbers, from 0 to 90 degrees.) This number is the zenith angle. To find the altitude angle, subtract the zenith angle from 90 degrees. This number will be the same as, or very close to, your latitude.
- Write down this number in your notebook.
- Take this reading several more times, noting the degrees in your notebook each time, to check for accuracy.
- Check your latitude against an atlas or a map.

create a world map in 1569 that portrayed an accurate picture of the spherical globe on a flat surface. He envisioned his map being useful for scholars, travelers, and seafarers.

Although a globe is the best way to show the relative positions of places, it was impossible to create a globe that could fit in the ship's cabin and provide the kind of detail necessary for navigation. Flat maps, on the other hand, are portable and can show a great deal of detail.

Mercator's most significant contribution to mapmaking—the one we remember him for—was his projection. He was determined to create a map where a navigator could draw a straight line between two points and determine the constant course he must steer in sailing between those points. These rhumb lines had been showing up on portolan charts for years but were only effective for plotting short courses, because the curve of the earth would throw the course line off. Mercator knew that the rhumb line had to be a long curved line. But how do you convert that to an easily plotted straight line on a map?

Mercator figured out that in order to straighten the rhumb line, he had to distort the map as it got further away from the equator. He spread the parallels

What explorer's expedition made the first circumnavigation of the globe?

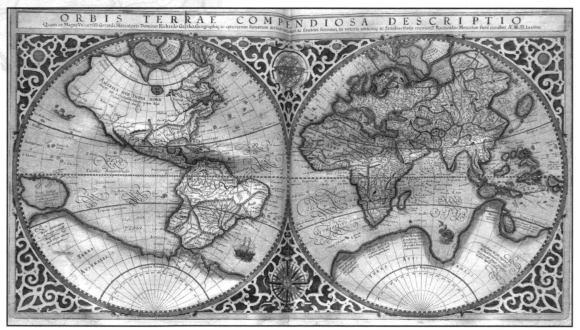

Mercator World Map.

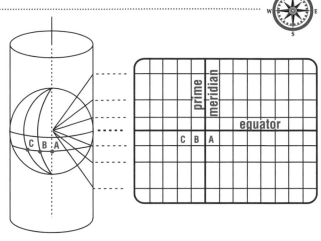

(the lines of latitude) at the same proportion as he spread the meridians (lines of longitude). For example, if at any place on the map a minute of longitude is spread to twice its value on the earth, then the corresponding minute of latitude is also spread to twice its value. All the lines of latitude and longitude are at right angles to one another (whereas in reality, the meridians would merge at the poles). This, basically, was the distortion formula for the Mercator projection.

What did this do to features on the map? Look at a map of the earth that's been flattened by Mercator's projection. Look at the size of Greenland. It looks huge! In reality, South America is nine times the size of Greenland. See if that proportion holds on the map you're looking at.

But Mercator's map projection worked. A navigator could plot a straight-line course to a distant land on Mercator's map. Although it would take a century before navigators would come to rely on maps projected this way, they would eventually become invaluable to ocean shipping.

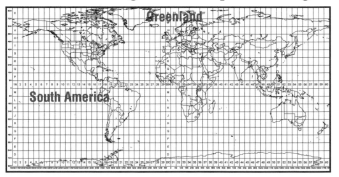

Over the years, cartographers have come up with various ways to project the sphere of the earth onto paper and each of these maps is used for very specific purposes. As you can imagine, each map projection has its own weakness as well because no single projection can accurately portray area, shape, scale, and direction.

Map projections come in two broad categories: conformal and equal-area. Conformal maps are preferred by navigators and engineers because they preserve the shapes of the small parts of the mapped surface even though they cannot

Example of a conformal map.

Example of a equal-area map.

preserve the shape of an especially large country or continent. A conformal map is useful for those trying to find the shortest route between two points. A Mercator projection is a conformal map (remember what happened to Greenland).

An equal-area map is used when a standard scale is more important than correct shape. These are preferred by scientists and geographers. On these maps, for example, one square centimeter on the map would equal the same number of kilometers on the map no matter where you are. Topographic maps are equal-area maps. The downside of an equal-area map is that it distorts shapes and distances.

How to Measure Longitude: the Chronometer

The marine chronometer (a sea clock) was the first precise instrument to figure out distance between two locations. How can a person figure out distance by measuring time?

When the chronometer was invented by the English clockmaker John Harrison in the late eighteenth century, astronomers and mapmakers had already calculated the size of the surface of the earth. This meant that it should be possible to figure out the distance between two locations on either land or sea, but in order to do that navigators needed something that would keep absolutely accurate

Chronometer known as H-1.
The first attempt by John Harrison.

WORDS TO KNOW

conformal map: *preserves both the angles and shapes of small figures.*

equal-area map: *the scale remains the same anywhere on the map.*

chronometer: *a very accurate portable clock used to determine longitude.*

International Date Line: *an imaginary north-south line at approximately 180 degrees in the Pacific Ocean; where each calendar day begins.*

Greenwich mean time: *the local time at 0 degrees longitude, the prime meridian.*

MEASURING DISTANCE

Distance was measured from the prime meridian located at Greenwich, England. This was also the starting place for measuring time. Remember that a traveler moving west from the prime meridian goes back in time (San Francisco, California, is eight hours earlier than London, England) and moving east from the prime meridian goes ahead in time (Osaka, Japan, is nine hours later than London, England). At the International Date Line, *the date changes so travelers don't gain or lose a day.*

There are 24 hours in the day—the earth turns on its axis 360 degrees, or in a complete circle, every 24 hours (and there are 360 degrees in a circle)—and if we divide 360 into 24 parts we find that the earth turns east toward the sun 15 degrees every hour, which corresponds to the lines of longitude drawn on many maps. For example, when the sun "passes the meridian" at noon, we only need to check Greenwich mean time. *If it is 3 pm in Greenwich it means it was noon three hours ago in Greenwich. Therefore we know we are at longitude 15 degrees x 3 hours = 45 degrees west.*

Here's the cool part: Since San Francisco is eight hours from London and we know that eight hours represents one-third of twenty-four hours we can assume that the distance from San Francisco to London (5,360 miles or 8,626 kilometers) is equal to one-third the distance around the earth at *that latitude. London's latitude is 51°32′N and San Francisco's is 37°37′N so you have to do a little math to figure the distance out exactly. Also remember there's a difference between nautical and statute or land miles (multiply a land mile by 1.15 to get a nautical mile).*

What is the difference between a conformal map and an equal-area map?

H-4 chronometer designed by Harrison.

time. Remember, distance could be calculated by multiplying the speed of the ship by time traveled. If the time was measured inaccurately, the calculation of distance could be way off.

In the seventeenth and eighteenth centuries, the "problem of longitude" assumed great strategic importance and occupied some of the best scientific minds. Why was this so important? Because France, Holland, and Britain were all competing for lands discovered during exploration and if a country was going to claim land, it had to be able to accurately describe where it was in geographic terms—by latitude and longitude. In 1714 Britain announced a prize of 20,000 pounds—a huge sum of money in those days—for a reliable solution to determining longitude, and John Harrison, a British clockmaker, spent decades trying to achieve it. His first two chronometers—or very accurate clocks—of 1735 and 1739, though accurate, were bulky and delicate pieces of machinery. Only his fourth instrument, tested in 1761, proved satisfactory. A marine chronometer had to be made in such a way that it could operate under terrible conditions.

While other clocks of that time operated on flat, level surfaces because they used pendulums, Harrison constructed his chronometer using a coiled spring to replace the pendulum. This allowed the clock to keep on ticking as it rolled from side-to-side and even while upside down! Harrison also discovered that if he made his chronometer from all brass parts that required no oil, his timepiece was resistant to temperature and humidity changes. This remarkable clock lost only a second or two per month.

Captain James Cook was the first navigator to use a marine chronometer as he accurately charted parts of the Pacific Ocean's coastline, including the islands of

New Zealand and Tahiti. By the early nineteenth century the British government was making sure every government ship had a marine chronometer on board and by 1850 each British naval ship carried three chronometers—one was permanently set to Greenwich mean time, one was set to the local time, and one was to make sure the ship always had the correct time even if one timepiece broke.

Captain James Cook (1728–1779)

Captain James Cook.

Captain Cook was a remarkable explorer and navigator during the second half of the eighteenth century. Because he was born into a poor farming family in North Yorkshire, England, Cook's many accomplishments seem even more remarkable for a day and age when wealthy men were much more likely to attain positions of power and authority.

He began his sea career as a teenager when he worked on ships carrying coal up and down the east coast of England. Sailing these treacherous waters provided Cook with invaluable experience in practical navigation. He joined the Royal Navy in 1755 and qualified to be a navigator within a couple of years. He spent the years after the Seven Years War charting the coast of Newfoundland, which gave him a practical grounding in the technical skills needed to be an effective explorer.

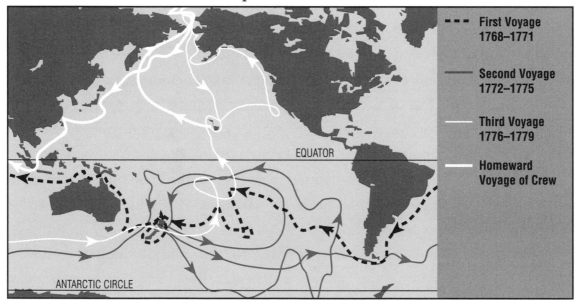

Map of the Pacific showing the routes of Cook's three voyages.

Who invented the chronometer?

.... *Chapter Three: The World Expands*

Captain Cook made three Pacific voyages. He was sent to Tahiti, a little-known South Seas island, in 1768 to make astronomical observations about the transit of the planet Venus. While he was there, he was also instructed to search for Terra Australis Incognita, the great southern continent. Up to this point, navigators and mapmakers had no idea what Antarctica looked like—but they knew some landmass lay over the South Pole. The Dutch had touched upon what we call Australia, which they called New Holland, but details about it were murky, at best.

From Tahiti, Cook sailed south to 40 degrees south where he turned west and sailed to New Zealand. He charted the New Zealand coasts and proved that they were not part of a great southern continent. He then charted the eastern and northern parts of New Holland, narrowly escaping from being slammed onto the

Cook nearing Terra Australis Incognita, or Antarctica.

Great Barrier Reef. By the time Cook returned to England, he had mapped more than 5,000 miles of previously unknown coastline in the Pacific.

Cook carried John Harrison's famous Number 4 marine chronometer on his second voyage, allowing Cook to accurately determine his longitude while at sea. This was a "test drive" for the newly invented marine instrument and it performed superbly. He again sailed for Tahiti and New Zealand and mapped Easter Island, the Marquesas Islands, Tonga, and Vanuatu. Many of these islands were known but they were not mapped. What Cook did in these two Pacific voyages was to meticulously chart and map—giving us the first modern map of the South Pacific.

During several months of Cook's final Pacific voyage (1776–1780) he mapped the northwest coast of America—from Vancouver Island to the Bering Strait—in an attempt to find a northwest water passage that would allow Europeans to sail more or less straight to Asia without having to round the tip of South America. William Bligh, of *H.M.S. Bounty* fame, served as a navigator on Cook's

Where is New Holland?

last voyage. Cook never did find a navigable northwest passage but once again did a remarkably accurate job of mapping the coastline.

Cook did discover the Hawaiian Islands (which he named the Sandwich Islands) and the northern Polynesian islands—previously unknown island groups to Europeans—on his way to the northwest coast of America on this last voyage. When he returned to Hawaii, trouble was brewing. Some of the native people believed Cook to be a god—and Cook didn't do anything to make them think otherwise. Cook set sail and left the harbor on the Big Island of Hawaii. Everything would have been fine, but he had to return to make repairs to his ship. When the native people saw Cook had come back, some of them became very angry because they realized that Cook was not a god, but rather just a man with problems with his ship. Cook was killed in a skirmish on the beach. The native people took his body and there are numerous stories about where his body—or parts of his body—finally ended up.

During Cook's remarkable career, he sailed over 200,000 miles—roughly equivalent to circling the equator eight times or flying to the moon. He redrew

WHAT WE LEARNED FROM CAPTAIN COOK

Cook's voyages were not only to map but to further our understanding of the natural world. He kept extensive journals of his voyages, noting and naming the many plants and animals collected from exotic places. His first voyage on the ship Endeavor *was to witness the transit of Venus and to make*

astronomical observations. On all of his voyages he insisted that his crew eat citrus fruit, or food rich in vitamin C, as a way to combat scurvy, which was a horrible disease that afflicted people on long sea voyages. Many were saved from wretched deaths by Cook's insistence on serving citrus fruit. Have you ever heard of British sailors being referred to as "limeys?" That's from eating limes or other citrus fruit.

the map of the world and embarked on the first recognized "scientific" journey. Cook expanded our knowledge of the geographic world, and his shipmates—including artists, naturalists, and astronomers—made observations and collected specimens, greatly expanding our knowledge of the natural world.

SEXTANT

In 1731, Thomas Godfrey and John Hadley independently invented the reflecting quadrant, a precursor to the sextant, and in 1757, John Campbell invented the sextant. Royal Naval Captain John Campbell's sextant could measure both longitude and latitude. The sextant was a sophisticated device for measuring the angle between two objects. It's made up of an eyepiece, two mirrors, a sixth of a circle (hence the name), and a movable arm. Sounds complicated but it's not. The objective is to be able to see the sun superimposed on the horizon, which happens when the sun and horizon are lined up in the mirrors. Then all the navigator did was read the measurement on the calibrated circle. This is called "shooting the sun."

This navigational instrument was small and easy to use on a rolling ship and to a gifted navigator like Captain Cook, it was an invaluable piece of equipment. The sextant was a wonderful navigational tool because of its accuracy. It can measure an angle to the nearest ten seconds of a degree, which could tell the navigator where he was within one or two miles. Sextants were only really made obsolete by modern navigational equipment. You've probably seen sextants being used in movies like Master and Commander.

WORDS TO KNOW

sextant: *an instrument used to measure how high the sun is above the horizon. The angle and the time it is measured can be used to calculate latitude.*

shooting the sun: *using a sextant.*

Name some citrus fruits.

LATITUDE AND LONGITUDE

Knowing latitude and longitude is a simple way to identify location. Navigators talk about their north-south position using parallels of latitude—the lines running across the map, chart, or globe, from left to right, west to east. A latitude coordinate tells how far north or south you are from the equator, the line that goes around the middle of the globe dividing it into the Northern and Southern Hemispheres. A longitude coordinate tells how far east

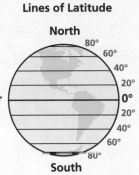

Lines of Latitude

North
80°
60°
40°
20°
Equator 0°
20°
40°
60°
80°
South

or west you are from the prime meridian, the line of longitude that runs through Greenwich, England. Lines of longitude, which are also called meridians, run north and south on a map and converge at the poles.

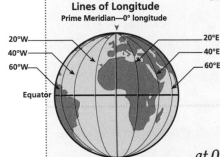

Lines of Longitude
Prime Meridian—0° longitude

20°W — 20°E
40°W — 40°E
60°W — 60°E
Equator

Distance is written in terms of degrees. The equator lies at 0 degrees and the parallels of latitude north of the equator are identified as north, and those south of the equator are identified as south. The North Pole lies at latitude 90 degrees north, and the South Pole at 90 degrees south. The prime meridian lies at 0 degrees longitude. Meridians of longitude east of the prime meridian are designated as east, and those west of the prime meridian are identified as west.

Where longitude 180 degrees west meets longitude 180 degrees east in the Pacific Ocean is the International Date Line, the place where the date actually changes. Fortunately the International Date Line doesn't go through any islands—it zigs and zags along the 180-degree meridian—otherwise for people living on one side of the date line it would be today, and for their neighbors living on the other side it would be tomorrow, which could get very confusing.

Without the International Date Line, travelers going westward would discover

Which ocean did Captain Cook explore and chart?

that when they returned home, they had spent one more day on their vacation than they thought, even though they had kept careful tally of the days. This happened to Magellan's crew after their first circumnavigation of the globe. Likewise, a person traveling eastward would find that one fewer day had elapsed than he or she had recorded, as happened to Phileas Fogg in **Around the World in Eighty Days** *by Jules Verne.*

Each degree of latitude and longitude is divided into 60 minutes, and each minute is further divided into 60 seconds (think of how time is divided and you'll never forget this). Navigators measure distance in nautical miles. One nautical mile equals one minute of one degree and has been set at 6,080 feet. So one degree of latitude or longitude equals 60 nautical miles (or 70 land miles).

Any location on earth is described by two numbers—its latitude and its longitude. If a ship's captain wants to specify position on a map, these are the "coordinates" they would use. Think of position coordinates like you think of street addresses. When position coordinates are given, it's just a way to pinpoint a place by identifying where lines of longitude and latitude intersect. This can be particularly helpful in the middle of the ocean where there are no visible

landmarks. Coordinates *are always read by stating the latitude first and the longitude second. One very famous set of position coordinates is latitude 41 degrees 33 minutes north, longitude 50 degrees 01 minute west. On April 14, 1912, this is where the ocean liner* Titanic *struck an iceberg in the northern Atlantic Ocean and quickly sank.*

WORDS TO KNOW

coordinates: *numbers that identify a position. Central Park in New York City is latitude 40°47'N, longitude 73°58'W.*

ACTIVITY

Measure Your Local Time

In order to properly determine longitude, explorers had to know the local time. Make a sort of sun dial with this activity to determine noon.

Supplies:

- One three-foot-long pole that you can hammer into the ground
- 15-inch-long string with a weight tied to one end
- Nine scraps of paper
- Nine pencils or sticks
- Yardstick or tape measure
- Protractor
- Notebook
- Pencil

Instructions:

- Choose a sunny location on a flat spot of ground—beware of shadows from buildings and trees.

- Set up the pole so that it is vertical. Check this by using your string as a plumb line—it will hang straight down—and align your pole with the string. Hammer the pole firmly into the ground so it will not move during the day.

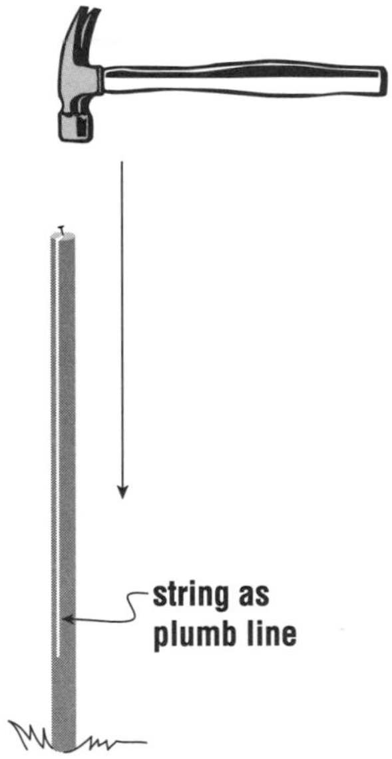

- Measure the height of the pole and record that in your notebook.

- Label your scraps of paper with observation times making symmetrical

string as plumb line

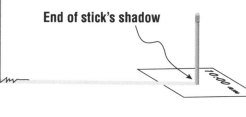

10:00 am

End of stick's shadow

observations around noon. Remember that daylight savings will delay local noon by one hour. Suggested intervals might be: 10:00, 11:00, 11:20, 11:40, 12:00, 12:20, 12:40, 1:00, 2:00.

- At the observation time, take the scrap of paper with the time written on it, poke the pencil through it and push it into the ground so that the point of the pole's shadow lines up with the hole where the pencil goes through the paper. Do this at each observation with a new paper and pencil.

- Measure the length of the shadow from the base of the pole to the pencil and record this number next to the time.

- Measure the angle between the shadow and the previously recorded position. Do this by using your string and stretching it from the pole to the previous pencil and then measuring the angle with a protractor. Record this in your notebook.

- Determine the time when the sun was highest—this is local noon. (Hint: A shadow will be shortest at noon.) Is this number different from what the clock says? Also, the shadow at local noon points to geographic north.

record this angle

Stretch string from pole to previous pencil

ACTIVITY

Circumnavigate the Globe

In this activity, you'll practice measurement and recording latitude and longitude on a global scale! And you'll also test your basic knowledge of geography.

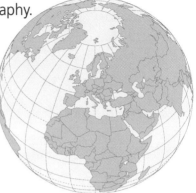

Supplies:

• World map or atlas with a scale

• Piece of string for measuring distances

Instructions:

• Begin and end your journey at Greenwich, England

• Circumnavigate the globe once.

• Visit every checkpoint destination as described in the clues.

• Visit the checkpoints in order (no backtracking).

• Record the name of the checkpoint, the distance traveled from point to point, and the latitude and longitude of each checkpoint.

Checkpoint Destination	Latitude and Longitude	Estimated Distance
1. Greenwich, England	lat 51°29'N, long 0°00'W	0 miles

2. See glaciers and volcanoes on this one little island in the North Atlantic.

3. Visit the capital of the United States.

4. Make a stop at an island nation once famous for premium cigars.

5. Visit an island made famous by Charles Darwin and the voyage of the *Beagle* (hint: be sure to travel through the Panama Canal).

6. Visit a group of islands that lie "midway" across the Pacific Ocean.

7. Stop at the capital of the Philippines.

8. Drop anchor in a city in Western Australia that's named after a city in Scotland.

9. Sail on to the large island nation off the east coast of Africa.

10. Make a stop at the city in Africa that has a population of jackass penguins.

11. Rest at an island group whose name includes the word for "green" in Spanish.

12. Return to home port.

What was the total distance traveled? Now convert statute miles to nautical miles (divide by 1.1508)

LAND EXPLORATION
JUNGLE, MOUNTAIN, AND DESERT TERRAIN, AND THE MAPPING OF THE AMERICAN WEST

People headed overland for many of the same reasons they headed out onto the open sea. Some were thrilled by the excitement of exploration, some were searching for riches that might lie in far-off lands, some were looking for the best route to get from here to there, and some were searching for new places to live. Typically, exploration would be financed by a government or company (like the Dutch East India Company) that stood to gain financially by whatever was discovered.

Try to imagine what some of the problems in navigating on land might be. We'll take a quick peek at what explorers ran into as they tried to make their way through the jungles, deserts, and mountains.

Jungles

Jungles or rain forests cover vast areas of the tropics near the equator. They're characterized

Meet Lewis and Clark

Improve your sense of direction

Map your school or backyard

Follow the Oregon Trail

as rainy, humid regions with layers of tangled, impenetrable vegetation (think about the landscape in any *Tarzan* or *George of the Jungle* movies you've seen)—people often have to hack their way through the undergrowth with machetes. When we think of jungle animals, we often think of the large mammals—like lions,

Dense foliage of a jungle.

tigers, and monkeys—but there are also creatures like snakes, alligators, and birds that add to the overall ambience of the place. And don't forget the many, many species of insects that can carry diseases like malaria, yellow fever, and cholera.

About the only way to really navigate in a jungle is by using the method known as dead reckoning—which means you have some idea of where you're going and how long it will take you to get there. With a map, a compass, and the knowledge of paces (how fast you can move through any kind of terrain and the distance you can then cover), it's possible to make your way through the jungle. Early jungle explorers would take advantage of trails created by animals—trails that often led to and from water—and if they got lost, they would follow a stream or river downstream because it would inevitably lead to a settlement or flow into a bigger river or the ocean.

Desert dunes.

Deserts

Navigating across a desert had its own set of problems. Think about it—the land is always shifting as the sand moves with the wind. About 5 percent of the earth's surface is covered by deserts—which are characterized by very little or no rainfall—including the big

Where do trails created by animals in the jungle typically go?

ones we've all heard about: the Sahara Desert in Africa and the Gobi Desert in Mongolia. Today, GPS makes desert travel much easier and has made the desert accessible to many people. But before the invention of global positioning satellites, nomadic people like the Arab Bedouins were able to travel safely through a most inhospitable landscape.

How did they do this? Nomadic navigators were very familiar with the position of the stars at night and they knew where the other stars were, relative to the North Star. During the day, they could determine direction by the shadows cast by the sun (this is sometimes called a sun compass). They also learned how to read the signs of the winds. Like the prevailing winds in the Mediterranean Sea, there are also prevailing winds associated with seasons in a desert. Learning

to read the patterns of the dunes and rock erosion due to prevailing winds could give valuable clues to direction.

Judging distances in a desert becomes very problematic because there are few reference points between the traveler and the horizon. The tendency is to think things are much closer than they really are (the dry desert air makes objects appear closer), so a good rule of thumb for inexperienced desert navigators is to multiply the distance it appears by a factor of three.

What is the most critical thing for all living things trying to survive in a desert? Water. Desert navigators often used camels for transportation because their bodies knew how to use water wisely. Navigators also learned to follow animal tracks and the flight paths of birds because these could eventually lead to oases and water.

An oasis in the desert.

Words to know

desert: *an area covered by sand characterized by very little or no rainfall.*

Why is it hard to judge distance in the desert?

BASIC GEOGRAPHIC TERMS

As we head on to land exploration, navigation, and map reading we need to understand some basic geographical terms. Geography vocabulary is important because many place names throughout the world include geographical terms (for example, Bering Strait, English Channel, the Gulf of Mexico, and Cape Cod).

Bay or Gulf—*part of an ocean, sea, or lake that extends inland. Bays are generally smaller than gulfs.*

Beach—*the sandy place where the water meets the land.*

Canyon—*a deep cut in the earth's surface through which water often flows.*

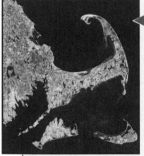

Cape—*a piece of land, generally pointed but often rounded, that juts into a body of water. Capes resemble peninsulas, but are often smaller.*

Cliff—*land that rises almost straight up from water or the earth's surface.*

Delta—*build-up of sediment at the mouth of a river where it enters a larger body of water.*

Downstream—*direction in which a river flows.*

Dunes—*hills or ridges of sand found on beaches and in deserts.*

Isthmus—*a narrow strip of land that connects two larger pieces of land.*

Lake—*a body of water surrounded by land.*

Left bank—*bank of a river or stream that is on one's left when facing downstream.*

Marsh—*soft, wet land with grass-like vegetation.*

Mesa—*flat-topped hill with steep sides.*

Mountain range—a series of mountains.

Pass—a low place through mountains or hills that allows for passage of people or vehicles.

Peak—the top of a mountain, usually pointed.

Peninsula—land that has three sides and juts into a body of water such as an ocean, sea, or lake.

Plain—a large, treeless, and fairly level area of land; generally flat, but may have low hills.

Plateau—a large, elevated area of land that is generally flat; may have some hills.

Pond—small body of water surrounded by land; usually smaller than a lake.

Rapids—place in a stream or river that has obstacles, such as rocks, over which water flows.

Right bank—bank of a river or stream that is on one's right when facing downstream.

River—natural and considerable water flow.

Slope—upward/downward slant on the side of a mountain.

Straits or Channels—narrow water passages between two pieces of land.

Stream—small, usually narrow, flow of water over the earth's surface.

Swamp—wet, spongy land with clumps of grass; some parts covered by water; some trees.

Trail to pass—the route one would follow to go through a pass.

Valley—a level area of land with upward slopes on each side; has the appearance of a V.

Volcano—cone-shaped hill or mountain with a hollow center from which lava and smoke flow.

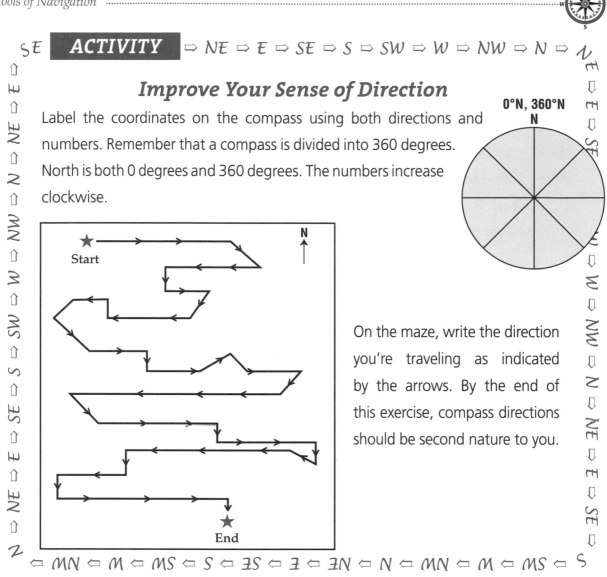

Improve Your Sense of Direction

Label the coordinates on the compass using both directions and numbers. Remember that a compass is divided into 360 degrees. North is both 0 degrees and 360 degrees. The numbers increase clockwise.

0°N, 360°N
N

On the maze, write the direction you're traveling as indicated by the arrows. By the end of this exercise, compass directions should be second nature to you.

Start

N

End

Mountains

Mountains tend to be grouped in ranges—like the Rocky Mountains in the American West or the Appalachian Mountains in the Eastern United States—or in a group—like the Adirondack Mountains in Upstate New York. No matter how they're arranged, mountains are often seen as obstacles to settlement. In the early nineteenth century, the United States government was determined to find a way through the Rocky Mountains,

Adirondack Mountains.

ANTOINE DE SAINT-EXUPÉRY (1900–1944)

I'm sure many of you have read The Little Prince. *In the story a pilot is stranded in the midst of the Sahara Desert where he meets a tiny prince from another world traveling the universe in order to understand life. During their conversations, the little prince discovers the true meaning of life and the aviator manages to fix his plane. Both the aviator and the little prince continue on their journeys.*

The author of The Little Prince *was a brave and fearless pilot in the early part of the twentieth century. Saint-Exupéry learned to fly at the age of 21. He became a mail pilot, delivering mail between remote parts of Africa and later in parts of South America. It could be very dangerous work because he was often flying over parts of the Sahara Desert where he would encounter fierce sandstorms, which would mean he was often "flying blind." This is when he learned to rely on dead reckoning—setting a course and knowing the speed of the plane and the time it would take to reach a destination.*

Saint-Exupéry wrote about his mail plane experiences in his book, Wind, Sand, and Stars. *He wrote, "Transport of the mails, transport of the human voice, transport of flickering pictures—in this century, as in others, our highest accomplishments still have the single aim of bringing men together." He volunteered to fly reconnaissance missions with an American P-38 squadron during World War II when one day, while on a mission, he just disappeared. No one knew if he had crashed or had been shot down. It remained a mystery until 1998 when a fisherman brought up part of a silver bracelet with Saint-Exupéry's initials on it while fishing off the Port of Marseilles. After recovering pieces of an airplane in 2004, sixty years after he vanished, the plane was identified as the one Saint-Exupéry had been flying.*

Did the engine malfunction? Was he shot from the sky? No bullet holes were found but because of the twisted wreckage, it appears that he fell vertically from a great height.

Saint Exupéry takes off on his last mission before disappearing.

TRIANGULATION

Triangulation is a technique for providing precise measurements of distances and angles that was developed by seventeenth-century explorers. It's based on the laws of plane trigonometry—if one side and two angles of a triangle are known, then the other two sides and third angle can be calculated. This is a bit abstract, but say you want to measure the height of a mountain. Think of the peak as one point on a triangle. You would measure the base of the mountain and call that the baseline. Then two adjacent angles are measured by using a surveying device called a theodolite, and with that information, you can construct the entire triangle. By constructing a series of adjacent triangles, values can be obtained for distances and angles not otherwise measurable.

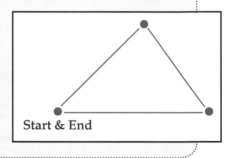

Start & End

which stretched from what is now Canada south to what is now the American Southwest. The government wanted to find a pass—or a way through the mountains—that would allow European settlers to expand to the Pacific (Native Americans already lived throughout the West).

What are the problems encountered by those trying to navigate through mountains? First, the change in altitude means that not only is it more difficult to climb or descend mountain slopes, but it will get colder as elevation increases. Travelers could find themselves totally unprepared to be making their way through the deep snow they might find on mountaintops.

In 1825 Jedediah Smith found the South Pass, a key passageway through the treacherous Rocky Mountains. South Pass had been discovered by earlier explorers and mountain men who worked

74

The South Pass.

OREGON TRAIL

This road to the West was known by many names. It was called the Oregon Trail, the California Trail, the Platte Trail, and the Mormon Trail by people who traveled it. It was primarily an emigrant trail. However, the Oregon Trail was also used by the Army, and stagecoaches and the Pony Express route followed part of the trail. The Oregon Trail continued to be heavily traveled during the Civil War, but once the Union Pacific Railroad was built in 1869, the use of the Oregon Trail declined.

Covered wagons along the Oregon Trail.

The Oregon Trail was an overland route from the Missouri River to the Willamette Valley in Oregon. The route had been used since early in the nineteenth century by trappers and traders, but the first wagon train of settlers reached Oregon by way of the trail in 1842. The next year came the "great migration," during which about 1,000 people and more than 1,000 head of stock followed the trail west. Within two years the number of migrants had tripled, and over the next decade, more and more families seeking homes in Oregon made the trek. The journey from Independence, Missouri, to the Willamette Valley took six months. This was a 2,000-mile trip where emigrants could experience hostile Indians, terrible weather, lack of food and supplies, and rough terrain. Do you think you could have made the journey?

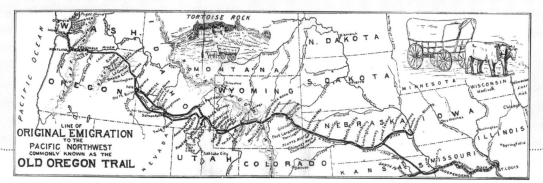

for the Astor Fur Company but its location had been kept secret. Smith made sure everyone knew about this important corridor. Running through west central Wyoming, South Pass was a 20-mile-wide break in the Rockies at the relatively low elevation of 7,550 feet above sea level. This is not a narrow notch—like we usually think of passes. In fact, most people using the South Pass didn't even realize they were crossing the Continental Divide (where the rivers on the western side of the divide flow to the Pacific and on the eastern side flow to the east).

This pass became the only practical corridor to the West. Beginning in 1843, a great migration of people—eventually up to half a million settlers—found their way to the western states by walking along what became known as the Oregon Trail. Once they found themselves in the South Pass, they still had 1,000 miles to go before they reached the Pacific. With prominent

Independence Rock.

landmarks like Independence Rock along the trail to help steer them in the correct direction, settlers made their way into western states like Utah, Oregon, and California.

Today, you can still see wagon ruts made 150 years ago by settlers moving through the South Pass in Wyoming.

Settlers who made their way across the United States did so searching for land and a new place to settle. These journeys were long and difficult and the settlers endured much hardship along the way. Settlers or pioneers would often be guided by men who were familiar with the trail, but that didn't prevent them from falling prey to harsh weather, hostile Native Americans, starvation, and wrong turns.

76

As the land became more settled, roads appeared along the paths taken by early settlers. Why? Because settlers were often guided along routes that contained the least number of obstacles. That meant people followed rivers and streams and looked for low places or passes—like the South Pass—to get through mountain ranges. Guides often followed paths made by animals or by Native Americans (who also followed animal paths). So when we look at settlement patterns, paths and then roads often appear on paths previously used by animals. People tended to create settlements along waterways for ease of travel and on good agricultural land where there was plenty of fresh water available. Look at the placement of some of the big cities in the United States—New York, Los Angles, Chicago, New Orleans—they're all on navigable waterways with good harbors in close proximity to fresh water.

Lewis and Clark Expedition (1804–1806)

On June 20, 1803, President Thomas Jefferson set the objective for the Corps of Discovery, as it would be called. Jefferson was interested in finding a northwest water route to the Pacific Ocean to open up the western wilderness to trade and settlement. He commandeered Captains Meriwether Lewis and William Clark to lead the expedition. Jefferson wrote:

> The Object of your mission is to explore the Missouri river & such principal stream of it as by it's course and communication with the waters of the Pacific ocean, whether the Columbia, Oregon, Colorado or any other river may offer the most direct & practicable water communication across this continent for the purpose of commerce.

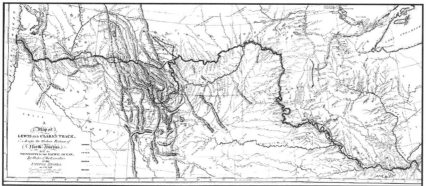

Imagine yourself in that time period. The known world of North America lay along the East Coast west to about Ohio. To venture

Map of Lewis & Clark expedition.

beyond was to go into the territory where Native Americans and fur traders lived and where stories about fantastic creatures (like wooly mammoths and gigantic bears) were told. But Lewis and Clark were both careful observers of the land around them, and Jefferson knew they would be able to map the territory they covered on the expedition.

LIFE ON THE TRAIL WITH LEWIS AND CLARK

Lewis and Clark recorded 122 animals and 178 plants previously unknown to science in their remarkable journals. Along with scientific observations, their vivid accounts of their life on the trail give us insight into what it was like to spend 28 months on the road in uncharted territory. The expedition had to be resourceful and brought along a sewing kit, carpentry tools, and a portable smithy.

Here are a few examples of life on the trail from their journals. Note the creative spelling.

July 30, 1805— ". . . having now secured my supper . . . I cooked my duck which I found very good and after eating it layed down and should have had a comfortable nights lodge but for the musquetoes which infested me all night . . ."

August 2, 1805— ". . . we feasted sumptuously on our wild fruits, particularly the yellow currents and the deep purple service berries, which I found to be excellent . . . on our way we saw an abundance of deer [and] Antelopes, of the former we killed 2. we also saw many tracks of the Elk and bear, no recent appearance of Indians . . ."

July 16, 1806— ". . . saw a buffalow & Sent Shannon to kill it this buffalow provd to be very fat Bull I had most of the Flesh brought on an a part of the Skin to make mockersons for Some of our lame horses . . . and put on their feet which Seams to relieve them very much in passing over the Stony plains . . ."

Images above: Pages from the journals of Lewis & Clark.

Meriwether Lewis

William Clark

Jefferson knew the importance of making measurements of latitude and longitude. He provided the expedition with costly mapping instruments including several compasses, a sextant, an octant, rods and chains (for linear measurement), telescopes, artificial horizons, drafting instruments, a very early version of a measuring tape, a chronometer, and books and tables giving the daily locations of the sun, moon, and planets to aid in computing geographical position.

Every day, for the 28 months of the expedition, Lewis and Clark made daily measurements of longitude and latitude, and calculated their course, the time, and the distance traveled. These they noted in their elk-skin journal under the headings "course," "time," "distance," and "remarks."

"Course" referred to the direction the expedition was traveling. They determined this by noting compass bearings between two points or two landmarks. For example, they might stand on a bluff and point their compass at a large rock jutting out of a hill a couple of miles away. This line between two points is called an azimuth. Their compasses registered magnetic north rather than geographic north so they also had to correct for the difference between the two (declination). As they moved farther west, they had to remember to constantly adjust the number they used for declination.

"Time" was the time required to get from the reference point used for the beginning of the azimuth to the end reference point. For example they would walk from the bluff where they stood and note how long it took them—in hours and minutes—to reach the large rock they took the reading from. They used a chronometer to get a precise measurement of time (that is if they remembered to wind it, which they periodically forgot to do).

WORDS TO KNOW

octant: *instrument eventually replaced by the sextant. Measures ⅛ of a circle or 45 degrees.*
forage: *search for food and provisions.*

How long did it take the Lewis & Clark expedition to reach the Pacific?

"Distance" was taking a measurement between the two points. This was either given as miles or as yards or rods. Measurements were obtained by pacing the course or by estimating the distance (knowing how much time it would normally take them to cover a particular distance by foot or by horse).

Journal map entry describing two forks of river.

The "remarks" were descriptive observations about the reference points and the surrounding countryside. For instance, they'd note how wide a river was at that particular point, and the height of the hills.

Journal entry describing encounter with Native Americans.

SACAGAWEA

As a young girl Sacagawea was taken from her Shoshone family by a raiding Indian party of Minnetares. She eventually ended up the wife of Toussaint Charbonneau, and accompanied him on the Lewis and Clark expedition. Sacagawea is only mentioned about 25 times in the extensive journals kept

by the expedition. But the picture that emerges is one of an incredibly resourceful young woman. She foraged for and taught Lewis and Clark about the nutritional and medicinal value of the native plants, proving to be very helpful to members of the expedition.

When they were near the headwaters of the Missouri River, in present-day Montana, Sacagawea became reunited with her Shoshone family, who she hadn't seen in several years. Her brother was now the chief of the tribe! She served as an interpreter and guide in that area of the northwest. Although Sacagawea clearly pulled her weight on this dangerous expedition—all the while caring for her infant son—she wasn't paid for her contributions.

Who was president during the Lewis & Clark expedition?

Their arduous journey took them through wild territory. Although they didn't find a water route to the Pacific Ocean, they did locate several passes that would allow settlers to cross the Rocky Mountains on their way to the Northwest. To help them speak to the Native American tribes they expected to meet along the way, Lewis and Clark hired Toussaint Charbonneau, a French trapper, to serve as an interpreter. Charbonneau brought along his wife, a young Shoshone woman named Sacagawea and their infant son, Jean Baptiste.

Photo of the Great Falls along the Missouri River.

Clark was responsible for creating the map that was engraved and published in 1814. Course and distance information is apparent on the map and coordinated positions are accurate to within 5 percent, an enormous achievement that wouldn't be surpassed until the area was mapped using aerial photography more than a hundred years later.

John Charles Frémont (1813–1890)

Lewis and Clark opened up the passage to the Northwest with their amazing expedition of 1804–1806. The United States government was very interested in finding out exactly what kind of land lay between the shores of the Atlantic and the Pacific Oceans. One of the more colorful characters who opened up the West to settlement by finding and then mapping easier ways to travel across the country was John Charles Frémont.

Frémont was the son-in-law of the powerful senator from Missouri, Thomas Hart Benton. Because of this connection, many believe that during some of Frémont's mapping expeditions, he was actually acting as a spy for the government. Secret meetings he had while in California in 1845 most likely led

81

Who helped Lewis & Clark communicate with the Native American tribes they met along the way?

ACTIVITY

Map the School Grounds (or Your Backyard)

This activity will give you some practical compass experience.

Supplies:

- Directional or orienteering compass
- Pencils
- Notebook
- Two large sheets of paper
- Ruler
- Yardstick or measuring tape

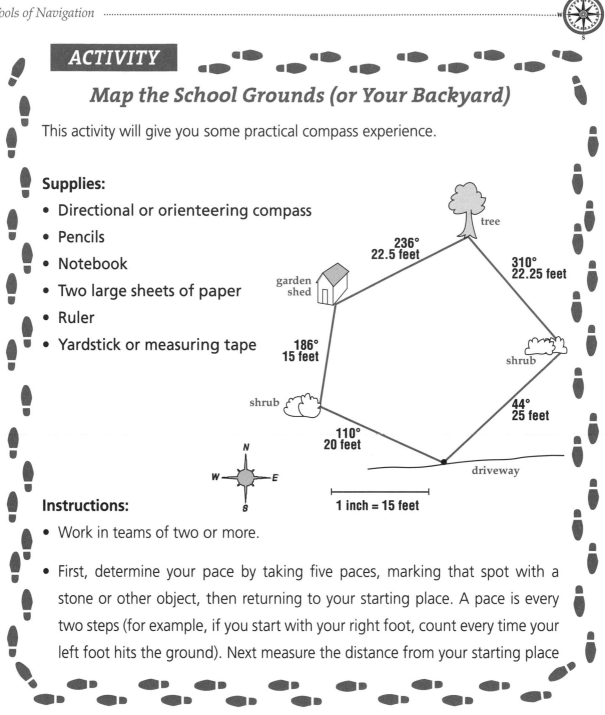

tree

236°
22.5 feet

310°
22.25 feet

garden
shed

shrub

186°
15 feet

shrub

44°
25 feet

110°
20 feet

driveway

N

W   E

S

1 inch = 15 feet

Instructions:

- Work in teams of two or more.

- First, determine your pace by taking five paces, marking that spot with a stone or other object, then returning to your starting place. A pace is every two steps (for example, if you start with your right foot, count every time your left foot hits the ground). Next measure the distance from your starting place

to the conquest of California, which was then a territory and part of Mexico.

What Frémont contributed to our knowledge of traveling to the West was maps. He was not an explorer; he traveled over routes that were already known. But by mapping them, he opened up many parts of the West to settlement. His

to your mark. Divide by five and that is your average pace. (Hint: your pace should be around five feet.)

- Determine the boundaries of your backyard or schoolyard. From your starting place, take a bearing on an object (tree, shrub, corner of a building) that's at the corner of one of your boundary lines. Write down that bearing in your notebook. Pace off the distance and write that down next to the bearing. Repeat this until you've determined the outline of your map. This is not easy and the more bearings you take, the more accurate your map will be. (Hint: only map the area you can see from your starting place.)

- Plot your bearings on your large piece of paper. Figure out what your scale is going to be, making sure your distances will fit on the paper. Try something like 1 inch = 10 feet. Find north from your starting place and draw a compass rose and scale on your paper.

- Place your compass directly on your paper and turn the compass housing to your first bearing. Next, line up the needle with the north arrow, which means turning the entire compass. Put a mark on your map where you are starting, then draw a line using the straightedge of your compass. Use your ruler to measure the line and extend it the proper distance.

- Plot all the bearings, always making sure to line up the magnetic needle with the north arrow. Label your lines with bearing and distance.

expedition of 1843–1844 mapped the Oregon Trail. He went to the Great Salt Lake and followed the Snake River toward Oregon and then headed south into California where he crossed the Sierra Nevada Mountains and then the Mojave Desert. In 1845 Frémont was surveying the Arkansas and Red Rivers at the

100-degree longitude boundary line of the United States when he went to the California territory and opened a new transcontinental route from the Great Salt Lake to northern California.

Frémont contributed to a government publication advertising the West as the place to settle. Then he acted as a guide for emigrants wanting to reach the West Coast. Frémont's maps of the Far West remained the most accurate depictions of parts of the frontier until the 1870s but exploration of the West was still incidental and haphazard throughout much of the nineteenth century.

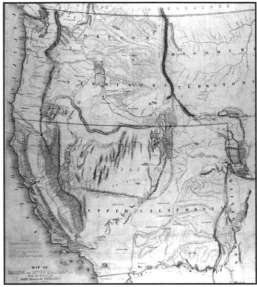

John Charles Frémont's route in 1845 would later become the Oregon Trail.

Even accurate maps were no substitute for good common sense for settlers moving west. The Donner Pass is a pass in the Sierra Nevada Mountains named for one ill-fated expedition where common sense did not prevail.

The Donner party was made up of 87 men, women, and children who made a terrible mistake when traveling across the country from Illinois to California in 1846–47. This group of emigrants decided to take a short cut that turned

The Donner Party is trapped by a snowstorm.

into a "long cut" that left them at the base of the Sierra Nevada Mountains at the end of October. With only 150 miles to go to reach Fort Sumter in California (now Sacramento), the Donner party became trapped by an early, fierce winter snow. They made lean-tos and crude cabins for shelter but food was scarce and the snow was too deep to hunt. Forty-one people died before they were rescued.

THE NEW AGE OF EXPLORATION
NAVIGATION FROM POLE TO POLE AS THE FIRST EXTREME SPORT

What spurred people to move west, away from the comforts of home and family? A couple of things. First was the promise of land. Many people wanted to leave the Eastern states, which were getting crowded, and find a place where they could carve out a new life. It was a very brave thing to do, especially since it meant traveling over thousands of miles with all of your belongings piled high in a wagon. While the oxen or horses pulled the wagon, all the members of a family would walk behind unless they were sick. Many people didn't make it and died while on the trail.

Have you ever heard the expression, "there's gold in them thar hills!"? The discovery of gold, silver, or copper in parts of California, Montana, Arizona, Colorado, and South Dakota brought hundreds of thousands of people to the West to try their hand at prospecting. Huge boom towns sprang up overnight whenever the cry "Gold!"

Meet the adventurers who conquered the highest peaks and traveled to the North and South Poles

Explore the great rivers of the American West

Discover Africa's remote corners

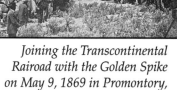

echoed through the land. Most who came seeking their fortune didn't find it, but once they were in the West, they stayed.

The government sent teams of engineers and surveyors west during the 1850s in what is known as the Great Reconnaissance. These surveying expeditions filled in some of the gaps on the map, providing an accurate and comprehensive look at the trans-Mississippi west. This was the first step to achieving a permanent link between California and the East—a link that would become a reality in the next decade.

In 1862, the building of the transcontinental railroad began. The Central Pacific line was laid from west to east over the Sierra Nevada Mountains, and the Union Pacific line was built from east to west, crossing the Great Plains and the Rocky Mountains. On May 10, 1869, to great fanfare, the two rail lines met at Promontory, Utah, permanently linking the two coasts. The connection of the two railroads bridged the 2,000 miles from the West Coast to the Missouri River. Try to imagine what an enormous task it was to lay down thousands of miles of tracks. The work was very hard and dangerous as construction crews blasted their way through mountains and built bridges over rivers.

Joining the Transcontinental Rairoad with the Golden Spike on May 9, 1869 in Promontory, Utah.

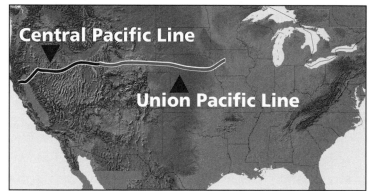

WORDS TO KNOW

Great Reconnaissance: *the period of western exploration just before and during the Civil War.*

trans-Mississippi west: *the frontier west of the Mississippi.*

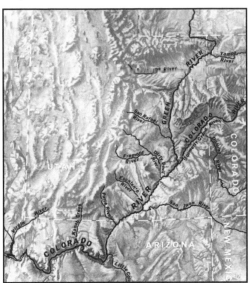

Map of the Colorado River.

The railroads hired very cheap labor—often newly arrived immigrants like the Chinese and the Irish—to do all the backbreaking work.

Even after the Great Reconnaissance there were still gaps in the map of the West. No one had mapped the Green River or the Colorado River (in modern day Wyoming, Utah, and Arizona) because that kind of mapping expedition was seen as too dangerous. These rivers cut deep canyons into rock, culminating in the Grand Canyon—the granddaddy of all canyons.

Although the Grand Canyon exposes rocks that are nearly two billion years old, the canyon itself is relatively young—only four to six million years old. The power of the mighty Colorado River cutting through the rocks of the Colorado Plateau as it has been rising up (due to a geologic process known as uplift) has produced a canyon one mile deep, 10 miles across, and nearly 300 miles long.

John Wesley Powell

In 1869, a one-armed Civil War veteran (he lost his arm at the Battle of Shiloh) convinced nine other men to set out from Green River Station in the Wyoming Territory on what is known as the Colorado River Exploring Expedition. John Wesley Powell, soldier turned professor of geology, intended to make scientific observations and map the region, filling in the blank space on the map.

The 10 men headed out in four boats with enough food for 10 months and their mapping equipment—compasses, barometers, chronometers, and a sextant. In addition to mapping the course of the rivers, they also planned to measure the height of the canyon walls.

This was a very bold, and some would say foolhardy, expedition. These men were trapped on the river for 99 days, traveling through areas with canyon walls

How deep is the Grand Canyon?

MEASURING CANYON WALLS

John Wesley Powell and his men used barometers to figure out altitude, or the height of the canyon walls. How did they do that? We think of barometers as tools for measuring changes in weather pressure. Because pressure changes with changes in altitude, barometers can also be used for this kind of mapping. Powell would have one man reading a barometer every half hour while sitting at camp, as he and another man climbed the canyon wall carrying a barometer, also taking readings every half hour. When they got back to camp, Powell could compare the readings that were done simultaneously. The difference between the readings would help him determine latitude. This was dangerous work and the men climbed without ropes or any safety gear. And remember, Powell had only one arm.

that were often so high or so sheer that there weren't places to pull the boats out and make camp. The mid-summer weather was miserable, and temperatures soared into the triple digits. But the most unpredictable thing of all was the river. The expedition never knew if rapids or a waterfall or still water lay around the next

Cliffs on the Colorado River.

bend. They would often hear rapids before they saw them, which added to the tension. Food became a preoccupation. There were few wild animals like deer or rabbits to hunt for food at the bottom of the canyon and much of their supply of food was eaten, lost, or spoiled in the first seven weeks of the trip.

By the end of the 99-day expedition, they had covered 1,000 miles of twisting, turning, white-capped water. They were down to six men from the original ten—one left at the first chance he got, and three climbed out of the

What groups of immigrants were important in the construction of the Transcontinental Railroad?

canyon just hours before the expedition ended and were never heard from again and were presumed dead. Two boats were lost. The group had run 414 rapids and portaged (carried their boats) around 62 others. At the end of the journey all they had left to eat was 80 pounds of coffee, 15 pounds of dried apples, and 10 pounds of flour.

These were the first white men to "run" the length of the canyon, and Powell's official government report of 1875 details the hardships they endured. But it also documents the marvels of the canyon—the extraordinary geology and the power of the river—some of which have been lost with the building of dams in the 1960s. It would be decades before anyone else would attempt to "run the canyon."

Exploring Africa: "Dr. Livingstone, I presume?"

Dr. David Livingstone

Across the Atlantic Ocean lay Africa—a large, mysterious continent with impenetrable jungles, fierce and wonderful wildlife, seemingly endless deserts, and exotic people. There are remarkable exploration stories about Africa, many connected to the search for the source of the Nile River. But Africa was also the source of the slave trade. This prompted many anti-slavery missionary societies to send missionaries to what was known as the "dark continent."

One of the most famous nineteenth-century missionaries to spend time in Africa was Dr. David Livingstone (1813–1873). A Scottish medical doctor by trade, Livingstone was also an ardent missionary and intrepid explorer. From 1840 until his death in 1873, Livingstone spent most of his time in Africa. He first crossed the Kalahari Desert in 1849, which people said

was impossible to do, and then took his family across the desert in 1851 (his wife became the first white woman to cross the desert).

Livingstone was driven to explore deeper and deeper into the vast interior of Africa, and

Dr. Livingstone, I presume?

in 1852 he set off from Cape Town on the Zambezi Expedition to explore and map the course of the Zambezi River. He stumbled upon and named Victoria Falls (named after Queen Victoria, Queen of England), a gorgeous drop of water located in modern-day Zimbabwe. Victoria Falls remains a popular tourist destination to this day.

SIR HENRY MORTON STANLEY

Sir Henry Morton Stanley (1841–1904) was born John Rowlands, in Wales. He took the name of an American merchant who gave Rowlands a job and virtually adopted him. Stanley was working as a newspaper reporter for the New York Herald *when his publisher sent him to Africa to find Dr. Livingstone, who had not been heard from for several years. Money was no object. Stanley hired 2,000 porters in Africa and set out for Central Africa. After eight months, Stanley found the ailing Livingstone in Ujiji and wrote in his journal that he greeted him with the now-famous remark, "Dr. Livingstone, I presume?"*

Map of the travels of Stanley and Livingstone.

Stanley nursed Livingstone back to health, and later accompanied him on an exploration of the northern end of Lake Tanganyika. Stanley spent the next decade exploring Central Africa, including leading a party down the lengths of the Lualaba and Congo Rivers to the Atlantic Ocean, which he wrote about in many books and articles. The party slogged and bushwhacked their way through brutal equatorial jungles where the expedition suffered from disease, desertion, drowning, and, at one point, an ambush by thousands of cannibals. Of the 359 people who began the expedition, only 108 reached the ocean. Although he made invaluable contributions to our knowledge about previously unexplored regions, Stanley was ruthless and brutal in his dealings with the African people.

Sir Henry Morton Stanley

Victoria Falls.

For four long years Livingstone mapped the midsection of the continent. His total journey was about 5,000 miles—and 3,000 of those miles were spent walking. He encountered malaria, dysentery, sleeping sickness, insect infestations, monsoons, and tribal wars. The horrors of the still-active slave trade he encountered on his journey made him determined to try to help the natives of Africa escape this horrendous fate, although his efforts were only marginally successful.

Exploring India: Mapping Everest

While gaps in the map of the American West were being filled in and Livingstone was walking across the African continent, the Great Trigonometrical Survey was taking place in India. Beginning in the 1830s, British surveyors started mapping the Indian subcontinent. By using the method of triangulation (explained on page 74) surveyors could accurately determine the heights of points above sea level. In 1844, the highest mountain in the world was determined to be 29,002 feet. This mountain was named Everest in 1865 to honor Sir George Everest, the man in charge of the Trigonometical Survey. Today the official height, set by the Indian government, is 29,028 feet. It is known as Chomolungma, or "Goddess Mother of the Snows," or "Mother Goddess of the Universe" to the Tibetan people. In Nepal it is called Sagarmath or "Goddess of the Sky."

The Himalayas—which means "house of snow" in ancient Sanskrit—stretch in a 1,500-mile curve across Southern Asia and consist of several parallel mountain

WORDS TO KNOW

malaria: *an infectious disease in sub-Saharan Africa transmitted by mosquitos.*

dysentery: *an infection of the intestines.*

monsoon: *a seasonal wind in southern Asia and Africa that brings heavy rain.*

Indian subcontinent: *large region in southern Asia, including Bangladesh, India, Pakistan, Sri Lanka, and parts of Nepal, Bhutan, and Myanmar.*

Who was Victoria Falls named after?

Mt. Everest, the highest mountain peak in the world.

ranges. Mt. Everest lies on the border between Tibet and Nepal. K2, the next highest peak at 28,250 feet, is also in the Himalayas and lies on the border between China and Pakistan.

From the early 1800s until 1949, Nepal was officially closed to foreigners. The Trigonometrical Survey employed local, or "pundit," explorers to do the surveying work in the Himalayas. These very brave men carried out their task in secrecy because they weren't supposed to be working for the British.

When word of the fantastically high peaks got back to England, there were people who wanted to climb them. This was a new breed of mountain climber, people interested in adventure and conquest rather than furthering science. They climbed with traditional equipment—crampons, ice axes, ropes, and woolen clothing—and were anxious to take on the Himalayas.

In 1922 the first Everest expedition was formed under the lead of Brigadier-General Charles Bruce of the British Army. No one knew what the effects of climbing almost six miles into the sky would be, so they took along crude, and

WHO ARE SHERPAS?

Sherpas are native to the mountain villages between Nepal and Tibet. Their villages are at 7,000 to 14,000 feet above sea level so they are naturally acclimated to the altitude. Sherpas have been accompanying climbers to the area for the past century and have shown amazing endurance and courage under the most difficult circumstances. The most famous Sherpa is Tenzing Norgay, who, along with Edmund Hillary, was the first to summit Mt. Everest in 1953.

Sherpa guide.

What do the Tibetan people call Mt. Everest? What do people in Nepal call Everest?

The Himalayas from space. Everest is the peak in the middle.

extremely heavy, oxygen equipment. They were accompanied by Sherpa porters who carried the equipment and provisions.

The Everest expedition made three assaults on the summit. At 26,700 feet, the climbers had difficulty breathing. They went back to a base camp and got oxygen containers and tried again. They made it to 27,230 feet but were turned back by fierce winds. On their third attempt they were stopped by an avalanche that killed seven of the Sherpa porters.

The British were determined to conquer Everest. In 1924, Englishmen George Mallory and Andrew Irvine made another attempt to summit the mountain. They each carried 30-pound oxygen packs after reaching 28,000 feet. Eyewitnesses say they got within yards of the summit and then disappeared. No one ever knew if they actually made it to the summit, or what happened. Several years ago, in 1999, climbers on Everest discovered Mallory's body, perfectly preserved in the ice and snow.

Mallory-Irvine expedition at camp. George Mallory and Andrew Irvine (back row left) and Sherpa porters.

The 1950s ushered in the golden age of climbing. Nepal had opened its doors to the outside world and climbers came in droves. In 1950, Annapurna, another Himalayan peak, was summitted by Maurice Herzog and Louis Lachenal. They became the first men to master a peak over 8,000 meters, at 26,545 feet.

In 1953, a British team led by John Hunt went to Everest. They established a base camp at 18,000 feet and another camp at 26,000 feet. From there a pair of climbers were chosen to attempt to summit. The first pair

The summit of Annapurna.

Do we know for sure who summitted Everest first? Who were the first known explorers to reach the summit?

were turned back by lack of oxygen. Then Edmund Hillary, a beekeeper from New Zealand, and Tenzing Norgay, a Sherpa, made their attempt. Hillary later wrote that he was preoccupied the entire time by their ever-dwindling supply of oxygen—he kept wondering if they would have

Edmund P. Hillary on the five dollar bill of New Zealand.

enough to summit and to return to camp. The climb was excruciatingly slow: they gained one foot per minute as they inched along. They finally made it. They stayed at the summit for 15 minutes where Hillary buried a small crucifix in the snow (at Hunt's request) and Norgay buried a packet of chocolate as a gift to the Buddhist gods.

Exploring the Poles: Race to Discovery

While continents were being explored and mapped and peaks were being conquered, there were two places on earth that held an endless fascination for

Dog sled in Arctic Alaska.

certain explorers—the North Pole and the South Pole. Both were extremely inhospitable places and one of them—the North Pole—wasn't even on solid land! Yet the race to the poles caught on like a fever and in the early part of the twentieth century the public was treated to harrowing accounts of Arctic and Antarctic exploration.

In the 1880s, Norwegian explorer Fridtjof Nansen had discovered evidence of a current that crossed the North Pole. A throwing stick used by the Inuit of the Bering Strait to kill seals was found in driftwood in Greenland, on the other side of the Arctic Circle. Nansen figured he could design and build a ship that could ride this "ice highway" across the pole. He left Norway in his ship, *Fram*, but got stuck in the ice for 35 months before breaking free and heading home, never having reached the pole.

What does the word Himalaya mean in ancient Sanskrit?

HOW DO YOU KNOW WHEN YOU'RE AT THE POLE?

Remember that your magnetic compass would be reading magnetic north but you want to get to geographic north. What would you do to figure out where you were going, particularly when the end of your journey was on ice that was moving? If you're standing at the North Pole, all points are south of you (east and west have no bearing). Since the earth completes a full rotation once every 24 hours, if you're at the North Pole your speed of rotation is quite slow—almost no speed at all, compared to the speed of rotation at the equator of about 1,038 miles per hour.

Arctic explorers carried a sextant with them to take measurements as they got closer and closer to the pole. Prior to GPS, this was the only accurate way to determine if you actually made it!

Magnetic Deviation

Magnetic North   **Geographic North**

The Arctic Circle begins at latitude 66°13′N and has at least one period of permanent daylight and one period of permanent darkness in a year. At 70 degrees there are no more trees anywhere. Above 80 degrees there are still bits of solid, permanently frozen land—the northern edge of Greenland, Ellesmere Island, part of Spitzsbergen, and Franz Josef Land—which is called permafrost. These are inhospitable places: extremely cold and barren. If you stood on the northernmost point of Greenland and looked toward the North Pole you would see only ice and water. The ice is always moving because of ocean currents and Arctic winds. This creates the pack ice—thousands of individual ice floes that are either thrust together, creating hills or pressure ridges, or driven apart creating rivers or Arctic lakes. The closer you get to the pole, the smoother the ice becomes.

Today the native peoples who inhabit the Arctic are called Inuit, although they were called Eskimos by the early Arctic explorers. In the early part of the

FRAM

Fridtjof Nansen proposed building a small ship (170 tons) that would carry five years of provisions for 12 men, would have an engine that could power the ship at a speed of 6 knots, and would be rigged for sailing. He called his ship **Fram,** *which means "Onward," and predicted it would take three years to cross the Arctic Ocean.*

The hull was designed so that the pressure of the ice would tend to push it up on the ice rather than crush it, as was the fate of the ships of previous expeditions. The sides were rounded, the bottom flat, and the ship one third as broad as she was long. In open seas, it was said, "She sailed with the smooth aplomb of an old barrel, but in ice she performed splendidly." Her hull consisted of three layers and was greater than 2 feet thick.

Fram.

twentieth century the Inuit lived by fishing and hunting and used sled dogs and sleds (sometimes called sledges) for transportation. They also used kayaks for fishing and hunting. The most successful polar explorers used the hunting and traveling techniques of the Inuit.

Salomon Auguste Andrée (1854–1897), head of the Swedish Patent Office and founder of the Society of Swedish Inventors, decided to conquer the North Pole by flying to it in a hydrogen-filled balloon. He figured it would take 43 hours to get there from Spitzsbergen. After several unsuccessful attempts to launch, he finally set off on July 11, 1897. Things

Arctic Circle

WORDS TO KNOW

Inuit: *native people who inhabit the Arctic.*

sledge: *a sled pulled by dogs used in the Arctic region for transportation.*

trichinosis: *the disease caused when the trichina larvae are transmitted through inadequately cooked meat.*

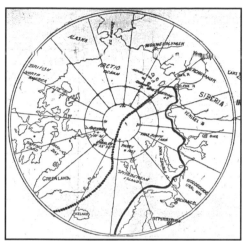

The dotted line shows Andrée's intended course; the solid line shows the places from which the balloon had been sighted.

went wrong immediately and he and his two companions had to throw precious provisions overboard to stay aloft. Three days later the balloon sank to the pack ice, and the expedition was never heard from again.

In 1930 a Swedish scientific expedition made an extraordinary discovery—they found Andrée's camp on White Island, a desolate spot 200 miles east of Spitzsbergen. Among the effects they found several diaries, which indicated the men survived until October 1. They also found a camera and were able to develop some of the photographs. It was originally assumed that Andrée and his men died from carbon monoxide poisoning by using their cook stove in a closed tent, but later it was determined that they actually died of trichinosis gotten from eating polar bear meat.

On April 6, 1909, Americans Robert E. Peary and Matthew Henson, and Inuits Egingwah, Seegloo, Ootah, and Ooqueah reached the North Pole. Peary wrote in his diary, "The Pole at last!!! The prize of three centuries, my dream and ambition for twenty-three years. Mine at last . . ." After 36 hours at the North Pole camp, the six men began the 413-mile journey back to land.

Peary had been trying to reach the pole for decades. He had spent time in Northern Greenland learning all he could from the Inuit—how to select the best sled dogs, how to drive the dogs, how to build igloos, and how to make clothes from the skins of animals like seal and polar bear. A Peary Arctic Club was formed

Robert Peary in the Arctic.

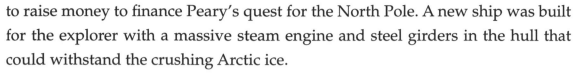

to raise money to finance Peary's quest for the North Pole. A new ship was built for the explorer with a massive steam engine and steel girders in the hull that could withstand the crushing Arctic ice.

Like many polar explorers, Peary left caches of supplies along his route. This way his sleds were lighter as he raced to the North Pole and he was guaranteed much-needed food and fuel on the return trip. Not reaching the caches or miscalculating their positions could mean the difference between life and death.

"The Pole at last!!! The prize of three centuries, my dream and ambition for twenty-three years. Mine at last . . ."

When Peary returned to land at the tip of Ellesmere Island, he discovered to his horror that Dr. Frederick Cook, another American, claimed to have reached the North Pole a full year earlier on

WHO WENT TO THE NORTH POLE WITH ROBERT E. PEARY?

Matthew Henson ran away to sea at the age of 12 and had already traveled the globe by the time he met Robert Peary in a Washington, D.C., hat shop where Henson worked as a clerk. Henson went on a Nicaraguan expedition with Peary and accompanied him on his trips to the far north. He became an amazing sledge builder, dog driver, and all-around assistant. It was believed that Peary chose Henson to accompany him on the final leg of the journey to the North Pole because Henson was black. That way Peary could claim to be the first white man to reach the pole. Today Matthew Henson is buried in Arlington National Cemetery a couple of yards from Admiral Peary. He is considered America's first black explorer.

Matthew Hensen

WORDS TO KNOW

cache: *a hiding place for storing and preserving provisions.*

Denali: *the highest peak in North America at 20,320 feet; means "the great one" in the Native American Athabascan language.*

The Times Herald

Mt McKinley Companion confesses . . ."It Was a Lie!"

Did He or Didn't He?

Famed Explorer Cook Nicknamed Dr. Deception.
His Claim of Reaching the North Pole Thrown into Doubt

Lorem ipsum dolor sit amet, conse ctetuer adipiscing elit, sed diam no nummy nibh euismod tincidunt ut la oreet dolore magna aliquam erat vo lutpat. Ut wisi enim ad minim venia m, quis nostrud exerci tation ullamc orper suscipit lobortis nisl ut aliquip

April 21, 1908. This became the biggest news story of the year—who actually reached the pole first? Cook's claim was soon thrown into doubt when the two Inuit who traveled with him said they never lost sight of land, which is over 400 miles from the pole. Then Cook's previous claim to fame—that he was the first man to summit Mt. McKinley (now called Denali) in Alaska—was exposed as a hoax.

But all was not smooth sailing for Peary. There were questions about the remarkable distances he covered in short periods of time. When questioned about his achievement by a Congressional committee, Peary had a difficult time explaining how quickly he traveled over short periods of time on his way back from the pole. He also couldn't explain how he managed to travel in a straight line on constantly moving sea ice from land to the pole without making any observations for longitude.

So how did Peary navigate to the North Pole when he had no stable landmarks for reference points? First, Peary knew that at local noon his shadow pointed due north. An hour later, his shadow would have shifted 15 degrees (and 15 degrees for all subsequent hours). When it was local noon, Peary set his compass course. Next he located an ice mass that lay along the compass course and then headed toward it.

Peary took chronometers, a sextant, and an artificial horizon with him on his trek to the pole. He was very capable of making accurate longitude determinations using the tools he had. Professional surveyors from the Coast and Geodetic Survey talked to Peary upon his return and were satisfied that he

Matthew Henson (front) and Robert E. Peary.

could accurately estimate longitude based on determining local noon. They then testified on Peary's behalf before Congress.

Today, most people accept that Admiral Peary—he was made an Admiral because of his trip to the pole—was the first white man to reach the North Pole.

Race to the South Pole

To the far south, another polar race began. Robert Falcon Scott, an Englishman, and Roald Amundsen, a Norwegian explorer, raced each other to see who would reach the South Pole first. Unlike the North Pole, which lies on shifting Arctic ice, the South Pole is on solid land—Antarctica.

One of the problems with exploring Antarctica was that no one lived there. This extremely inhospitable frozen land with mountain ranges and huge thicknesses of glacial ice was home only to birds and sea mammals. There were no native peoples like the Inuit to aid the explorers in their quest for the pole.

Amundsen (left) and Scott (right)

Amundsen had already had plenty of polar experience. Between the years of 1903 and 1906, he became the first man to successfully navigate the Northwest Passage, a famous sea route between Canada and Greenland that connected the Atlantic and Pacific Oceans. On this trip he spent many months on King William Island performing various scientific experiments and taking scientific measurements of the precise location of the magnetic North Pole. During this time the magnetic North Pole moved through this area. His Arctic experience led him to embrace the Inuit way of dressing—loose layers of clothes made from the skins of Arctic animals like polar bear and seal—and traveling. He understood the

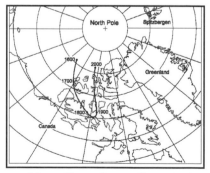

Magnetic north over the centuries.

What is the other name for Mount McKinley?

NORTHWEST PASSAGE

From the time Europeans first set foot in the New World they were determined to find a water passage to the west. They thought they should be able to travel from Europe to the Far East by traveling west, without having to go all the way around South America. Many explorers searched for what became known as the Northwest Passage, including John Cabot, Henry Hudson, William Baffin, John Ross, and John Franklin. Even Lewis and Clark were searching for a navigable waterway to link the East with the West.

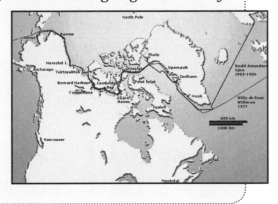

importance of having top-notch sled dogs and experienced sledge drivers.

Scott, on the other hand, was English to the core. He dressed in woolen clothing, which was no match for the unbelievably harsh Antarctic weather. When he left to cross Antarctica in 1910, he knew he was racing Amundsen for the honor of being the first to reach the pole. In the hope of making better time, Scott decided to use Manchurian ponies to haul his sleds. This was a bad idea because, even though they were used to a cold climate, these ponies could not withstand the howling winds and frigid temperatures of Antarctica. That left Scott and his men to haul the sledges themselves. On January 1, 1912, Scott was 170 miles from the South Pole. He decided to take four men with him on the final push, even though one man didn't have skis, which further slowed down and complicated the expedition.

On January 12, 1912, Scott finally reached the South Pole where he found Amundsen's tent and a letter addressed to Scott which read:

> *Dear Captain Scott—As you probably are the first to reach this area after us, I will ask you to kindly forward this letter to [Norwegian] King Haakon VII. If you can use any of the articles left in the tent please do not hesitate to do so. The sledge left outside may be of use to you. With kind regards I wish you a safe return. Yours truly, Roald Amundsen.*

WHERE EXACTLY IS THE SOUTH POLE?

Like the geographic North Pole, the South Pole lies at the point where the lines of longitude converge (it's like the part of the orange where all the sections come together). How would you know if you've actually reached the South Pole? As at the North Pole, you would use a sextant to measure the angle of the sun off the horizon. When Amundsen reached the South Pole he sent three men out at 90 degrees to each other with the instructions to travel 10 miles in those directions and to plant a flag. That way he knew he had encircled the pole. Amundsen stayed at the pole so that his team could take a series of hourly observations with the sextant over a 24-hour period to determine their actual position. They found they were 6 miles from the pole so they moved their camp.

Amundsen had reached the pole on December 14, 1911. This was a terrible disappointment to Scott but he couldn't dwell on that at the moment. He decided he had to leave on the 800-mile return trek the very next day because he was concerned for the health of his men. They never made it back. On March 21, 1912, Scott and his remaining two companions were holed up in a tent, pinned down by a blizzard. They were starving and freezing, and they knew they were not going to make it back. Scott's journal records those sad final days. Tragically, they were only 11 miles from a food cache when they died.

The Shackleton Expedition

Ernest Shackleton wanted to be the first man to cross Antarctica from the Weddell Sea in the north to the Ross Sea in the south. He sailed from England on his ship, *Endurance*, in 1914, just days after the beginning of World War I. In January 1915, *Endurance* became trapped in the pack ice. The crew stayed on the ship until October, when she was finally crushed by the ice. Some amazing photographs taken by the ship's photographer exist of

Ernest Shackleton

What did the Inuit make clothes out of?

Endurance *in the ice.*

Endurance as she sat stuck in the ice.

The crew salvaged what they could from the ship, including life boats, and then camped on an ice floe for the next three and a half months. They knew they had to head for solid land so they set sail in the lifeboats for Elephant Island, a barren rocky island 100 miles away. It became clear that no one would be looking for them—they would be presumed dead by that point—so they made a decision. Someone had to head for South Georgia Island—870 miles away—to get help from the whaling station there.

Shackleton and five men boarded one of their salvaged life boats, which was only 23 feet long and 7 feet wide, and headed out onto the treacherous sea. Seventeen days later, after enduring almost unceasing gales and even a hurricane, they landed on the remote, but inhabited, island of South Georgia.

LIFE IN ANTARCTICA

Surviving in Antarctica is extremely difficult. The largest land animal there is an insect, so the men of the Endurance *had to rely on seals and penguins and whatever they could catch in the sea for their food. There is no wood for fuel so blubber was burned. Although Antarctica is surrounded by water, by definition it's a desert (it has very, very low precipitation) so fresh water was an issue. During the summer months, ponds of fresh water would occur on top of the ice. Sea ice that has been above the water level for a while tends to lose most of its salt, so Shackleton's men could melt that. Keeping warm and dry took a lot of thought and energy and could be a matter of life and death. They were also dealing with shifting ice—cracks in the ice could occur at any time—and sometimes howling, blinding storms. It was also important to avoid prolonged exposure to the sun or snow because of the risk of eye damage from ultraviolet rays.*

What did Robert Falcon Scott find when he arrived at the South Pole?

South Georgia Island ▼

Elephant Island

How did they do it? They had a remarkable navigator on board, Frank Worsley, who kept them on course even though he could only take four sightings with his sextant over the course of the 17 days at sea. But their journey wasn't over yet.

The men had landed opposite the inhabited side of the island. They were going to have to cross 150 miles of mountainous terrain on foot before they reached the whaling station. With a compass, a chronometer, a cook stove, three days provisions, and 50 feet of rope, the men headed out.

When they finally staggered into the whaling camp, the whalers couldn't believe their eyes. Shackleton and his men had long been given up for dead. Twenty weeks after Shackleton headed out on his amazing journey from Elephant Island to South Georgia Island, he returned to collect his remaining shipmates, who were near death. Remarkably, during this entire time, not one crew member from *Endurance* was lost.

There were several other Arctic and Antarctic firsts in the early twentieth century that made our world seem just a little smaller. Admiral Commodore Richard E. Byrd flew a plane over the North Pole in 1926 and over the South Pole in 1929. Byrd became the best-known explorer of his generation. Amundsen flew a dirigible over the North Pole in 1926 and had a lifelong argument with the Italian designer of the dirigible, Umberto Nobile, as to who could actually claim the accomplishment. (Ironically, Amundsen died while searching for Nobile, his bitter enemy, when he was missing on another Arctic expedition.) Aerial exploration altered our view of the world from the North Pole to the South Pole and gave us a new perspective of our earth.

Admiral Commodore Richard E. Byrd

Who was the first explorer to reach the South Pole?

TWENTIETH CENTURY NAVIGATION

AERONAUTICAL NAVIGATION AND THE GPS REVOLUTION

Like sailors on the sea or travelers on the road, a pilot's job is to reach his destination. Just think about what the word "aeronautical" means—sailing through the air. This requires that pilots know their exact location at any point during the journey. To aid in this, pilots use compasses and other instruments to navigate accurately. Today, many airplanes are equipped with sophisticated computer equipment to make navigating a breeze, particularly on a long flight.

Learn how pilots navigate

See how GPS works

Discover how navigators find their way without using their eyes

Explore Mars on a Mars Rover

Flight Navigation

The aeronautical chart is the most important navigational aid to pilots. Published by the U.S. Department of Commerce, these charts look like road maps. They show the locations of various landmarks, airline routes, landing

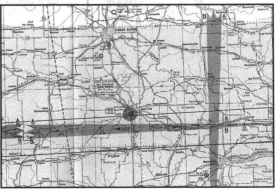

Detail of aeronautical chart.

fields, and radio stations that broadcast airplane navigation signals. The Instrument Flight Rules (IFR) chart is a special type of aeronautical chart that gives only the locations and frequencies of radio stations.

American airline pilots have to operate under instrument flight rules at all times. Airplanes carry a special type of radar receiver and transmitter called a transponder. The transponder receives a radar signal from one of a series of air route traffic control centers that are operated throughout the United States. When the signal reaches the ground, it makes the plane show up clearly on the radar screen allowing the traffic control centers to track the plane's progress.

If you've ever spent much time flying, chances are you've been stuck sitting on a runway at least once, waiting for the plane's turn to take off. Large and medium-sized airports have air traffic control towers where specially trained air traffic controllers use radar and radio communications to direct the planes that are landing or taking off. Many airports also have an instrument landing system (ILS) to help pilots land their planes safely. A series of radio beams from the ground operate a special instrument in the cockpit of a plane. Pilots can tell their exact position in relation to the runway by watching this instrument.

? WORDS TO KNOW

transponder: *a radar receiver and transmitter carried by all airplanes in America that allows airport traffic control centers to keep track of all the planes.*

air traffic controller: *someone who works as part of the air traffic control system to maintain a safe and orderly flow of air traffic so there are no mid-air collisions.*

VHF: *stands for very high frequency, used in FM radio, TV broadcasts, and aircraft communications.*

There are three main ways to navigate a plane, and most pilots use a combination of the three methods.

The simplest method is called piloting. Before takeoff, a pilot draws a course line on the aeronautical chart and keeps on the desired course by noting various landmarks. As the plane flies over each landmark—like a bridge, a highway, railroad tracks, a river, or a town—the pilot checks it off on the chart. If the plane doesn't pass directly over a landmark that lies along the course line, the pilot knows the plane is off-course and must be corrected.

Charles Lindbergh with his plane.

Another method of navigating is one you've already read about—dead reckoning. A pilot uses dead reckoning any time landmarks can't be seen, such as when flying over large bodies of water, forests, deserts, or through thick clouds. To navigate with this method, a pilot needs an aeronautical chart, an accurate clock (chronometer), a compass, and a small computer for figuring out complicated mathematical problems. The pilot plots the course on the chart in advance and figures out how long it should take to reach the destination while flying at a constant speed. Using the computer, the pilot can adjust the course to allow for the effect of the wind.

While in the air, the pilot uses the compass to keep the plane on course and keeps careful track of the time. Dead reckoning doesn't always work because winds can change and keep a plane from staying exactly on course. Charles Lindbergh used dead reckoning when he made his historic nonstop flight over the Atlantic Ocean in 1929. He plotted his course from New York to Ireland using Weems curves (see next page) and then flew through the night using only the stars and a compass to guide his way.

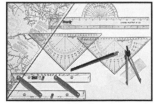

Navigation tools developed by Weems.

What are the three methods used by pilots to navigate a plane?

CAPTAIN PHILIP VAN HORN WEEMS

Captain Weems, nicknamed "the Grand Old Man of Navigation," was an innovator credited with vastly improving navigational techniques that had remained unchanged since the early 1800s. Weems was a brilliant navigator in the U.S. Navy who realized that if man was going to conquer the skies, they were going to have to figure out a better way to navigate. A compass, sextant, and charts were the necessary tools for plotting a course but these became very cumbersome in a cramped airplane cockpit.

Captain Weems, the Grand Old Master of Navigation.

In the early 1930s, Captain Weems invented the Second Setting Watch, which had an inner rotating dial that allowed the second hand to match the dial perfectly. This made finding Greenwich mean time (GMT) easier. In the air, a miscalculation in seconds could mean the difference between life or death. Weems also invented the Weems Plotter, which combined a protractor, a straight edge, and a parallel rule and is still one of the most basic tools for any navigator or even recreational boater.

His most significant navigational innovation was the simplification of a practice that provided an accurate fix from the position of the stars, sun, moon, and planets. He created pre-figured, quick-reference tables that eliminated or reduced the complicated mathematical computations required when taking a fix on a celestial body. These pre-calculated position lines were called Weems curves.

A teacher at the U.S. Naval Academy in Annapolis, Maryland, in the 1920s, Weems went on to establish his own school in Annapolis to teach the Weems System of Navigation. In 1928, Charles Lindbergh studied with Weems before attempting his history-making transatlantic flight. Admiral Byrd, who explored the North and South Poles in the 1920s, came to Weems for instruction before setting out on his Arctic exploration.

Radio navigation, the third method of navigating, is used by almost all modern pilots. Aircraft are equipped to receive signals from the more than 400 VHF (very high frequency) radio stations around the country. Pilots check their aeronautical charts to see what radio station they should tune to in a particular area and then set their equipment to receive this station's signal. A needle on the navigation equipment—called VOR (Very high frequency Omnidirectional Range)—tells the pilot when the plane is on a direct course to or from the station. When a plane drifts off course, the pilot can correct its direction.

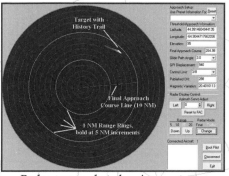

Radar screen shot showing contacts.

Boats and planes use radar to detect potentially dangerous unseen objects and to navigate near landmarks and land. We've all seen radar scanners in the movies. This is how it works. A radio pulse is sent out by a radio instrument through a rotating antenna, called a scanner. When the pulse hits a target, it bounces back to the scanner. The instrument calculates the time difference between transmission and reception. It converts this information into a visual display on a monitor called a scope, which shows the object as a point of light called a pip. The scope displays the bearing to the pip and its distance away—the location of the object relative to the radar unit. Radar can even track the movement of objects. This information is used to quickly produce accurate estimated positions and fixes. Radar is especially effective for ships and boats navigating narrow channels or areas that have many obstructions.

Special methods have been developed for navigating over long distances and across oceans. The two most common methods are inertial guidance and LORAN. Planes using inertial guidance have a computer and special devices that guide

? WORDS TO KNOW

scope: *a radar viewing monitor.*

pip: *a radar echo, a spot on a radar screen, that shows the position of a reflecting object. Also called a blip.*

inertial guidance: *guidance of an aircraft or spaceship using the instruments that measure direction and speed and a computer to maintain a predetermined course.*

GYROSCOPES

Most of you have probably played with a spinning top. A gyroscope is based on this same principle. An eighteenth-century English scientist, John Serson, noticed that a spinning top had a tendency to remain level even when the surface upon which it was spinning was tilting. He suggested that sailors could use it as an artificial horizon on ships. Unfortunately, when Serson went to sea to test this idea, the ship sank and everyone was lost, including himself.

León Foucault

By the mid-nineteenth century, the spinning top acquired the name, "gyroscope," though not through its use as a navigation tool. The French scientist León Foucault named his spinning top a gyroscope, from the Greek words gyros *(revolution) and* skopein *(to see); he had used it as a visual demonstration of the earth's rotation.*

A gyroscope.

In the early twentieth century, Elmer A. Sperry developed the first automatic pilot for airplanes using a gyroscope and installed the first gyrostabilizer to reduce roll on ships. While gyroscopes were not initially very successful at navigating ocean travel, navigation is their predominant use today. They can be found in ships, missiles, airplanes, the space shuttle, and satellites.

a plane on a predetermined course. Planes using LORAN have equipment for receiving special radio signals that are sent out continuously from transmitting stations. The signals indicate a plane's exact location.

The inertial guidance system of navigation is pretty neat because it's not only used to guide airplanes; it's also used on rockets, submarines, space shuttles,

WORDS TO KNOW

gyroscope: *a spinning disk or wheel that spins freely on its base regardless of any movement of the base.*

Inertial navigator measures this angle to determine the distance between Points A & B

Point B

Earth's Center

Point A

and missiles. Inertial guidance does not rely on any outside observations. A pilot doesn't have to know about the stars or landmarks or know where to pick up radio or radar signals, rather, the vehicle is guided by instruments. How do inertial guidance systems work? Gyroscopes indicate direction, accelerometers measure changes in speed and direction, and with this information, a computer constantly calculates the vehicle's position and guides it on its course. Together, these instruments are called the inertial navigator.

The inertial navigator measures how far a plane has traveled by keeping track of changes in the position of a vertical line. This line indicates direction to the center of the earth. Imagine two points on the earth's surface. Now draw lines through those points and have them meet at the earth's center. The inertial navigator measures the angle between the lines, which indicates the distance between the two points. As we've learned before, each minute (one-sixtieth of a degree) of angle represents a distance of one nautical mile (6,080 feet). For example, New York City is 3,006 nautical miles from London, England. A pilot flying from New York to London knows the plane has traveled far enough when the vertical line of the inertial navigator has moved through an angle of 3,006 minutes, which is 50 degrees, 6 minutes.

Inertial guidance acts as an automatic pilot. It is so accurate that it helps a pilot land an aircraft in poor visibility conditions. Many types of military craft, including guided missiles, submarines, and army tanks, employ inertial navigation systems. The military likes inertial navigation because the system cannot be jammed or sabotaged externally using existing military technology.

German scientists first used an inertial guidance system to guide their V-2 rockets against England during World War II. In 1958, two U.S. submarines used inertial navigators to navigate them under the Arctic ice to the North Pole. Today, many submarines, missiles, space shuttles, and aircraft are equipped with inertial navigators. They're even in some land vehicles, like tanks.

German V-2 rocket launch (above) and mobile launcher.

The other common method of navigating over long distances and across oceans, LORAN, is an acronym for Long Range Navigation. LORAN works by measuring the time difference in reception of radio signals sent by remote transmitters. The type of LORAN in use today is LORAN-C, where pairs of land-based transmitters simultaneously send radio signals toward each other. Special onboard LORAN receivers intercept these signals, then calculate position by measuring the difference in the time of reception. If a plane lies exactly halfway between the two stations (the centerline), there is no time difference between reception of the two signals. But anywhere else, the plane receives one signal before the other signal. The receiver converts the time difference between signals into a line of position. With two or more pairs of transmitters, the plane's position can be fixed and displayed in latitude and longitude. From the 1970s to today, LORAN-C has been the principal form of electronic navigation. In the future, it may be phased out because of widespread use of the Global Positioning System, or GPS, which uses a satellite network to determine location. Before GPS could be invented, though, rockets were essential.

WORDS TO KNOW

acronym: *a word formed from the initial letters of a multi-word name, like GPS.*
Sputnik: *a series of Soviet satellites, from the Russian words for fellow traveler.*

What does GPS stand for?

The Age of Rocketry

A great leap in navigation occurred during and after World War II. In a top-secret

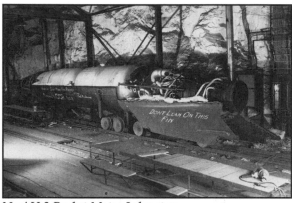

Nazi V-2 Rocket Motor Laboratory

German military laboratory in the tiny fishing village of Peenemünde on the Baltic Sea, 20,000 scientists, engineers, technicians, and workers perfected a number of weapons based on rocketry. The V-1 (also known as the doodle-bug or the buzz-bomb) was propelled by a jet engine and could travel 150 miles at 360 miles per hour. The direction was regulated by a magnetic compass and

a clock mechanism. The V-2, or guided missile, was the first modern rocket. It rose at a 45-degree angle on a trajectory that carried it 60 miles above the earth. The V-2 burned alcohol and liquid oxygen, and could travel a distance of 200 miles; gyroscopes guided it.

The Germans destroyed the rocket lab when the Russians advanced toward the area, and many of the scientists, including a young engineer named Wernher von Braun, surrendered to the Americans, transferring this knowledge to the fledgling American rocket program

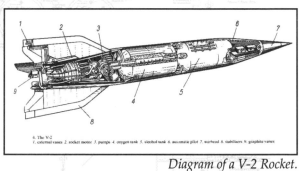

Diagram of a V-2 Rocket.

In 1957 the Soviet Union (now Russia) shocked the world when they launched Sputnik, the first satellite, into space. This was followed by Sputnik 2 one month later, which carried the dog, Laika, and Sputnik 3 six months later, which carried scientific equipment. The space race between Russia and the United States was on!

By 1961, 42 satellites had been launched into space—9 by Russia and 33 by the United States. On April 12, 1961, Soviet

Sputnik.

What was the first satellite launched into space named?

cosmonaut Yuri Gagarin became the first man to orbit the earth. His flight lasted 108 minutes. Within weeks, Alan Shepard, Jr. became the first American to be launched into space. His flight lasted just 15 minutes. Nine months later, on February 20, 1962, John Glenn orbited the earth three times in a 4-hour, 55-minute-long space flight. Glenn's spacecraft, Friendship 7, reached a maximum speed of 17,549 miles per hour.

By the end of the 1960s humans would walk on the moon, and now, decades later, there is an international space station used by scientists from around the world. We have also gone further and further from earth with probing, deep-space flights to Mars,

Apollo 11 astronaut Edwin Aldrin facing the U.S. flag on the lunar surface.

Venus, Saturn, and Jupiter. In the past half century, we've gained remarkable insight about not only the world we live on, but the universe we live in.

The GPS Revolution

In 1960 the United States Department of Defense started exploring ways to increase the accuracy of ballistic missiles launched from submarines. Out of this came the development of the Global Positioning System, or GPS. The whole system became fully operational in 1995. GPS works because there are 24 satellites orbiting the earth at about 11,900 miles above the surface. Each satellite is in a very precise orbit and goes around the

A ballistic missile on the launch pad.

Words to know

ballistic missile: *a missile that is guided in the first part of its trajectory, but falls freely at the end.*

Universal Transverse Mercator: *a geometric coordinate that is an alternative to using latitudes and longitudes. The advantage is that measurements are in meters rather than degrees.*

Who was the first American to go into space?

GPS GROUND STATIONS

There is a GPS master control station near Colorado Springs, Colorado, located at the Schriever Air Force Base, with five unstaffed monitor stations and three ground antennas located throughout the world. The monitor stations track all GPS satellites in view and collect ranging information from the satellite broadcasts, then send the information they collect from each of the satellites back to the master control station, which computes extremely precise satellite orbits. The information is then formatted into updated navigation messages for each satellite. The updated information is transmitted to each satellite via the ground antennas, which also transmit and receive satellite control and monitoring signals.

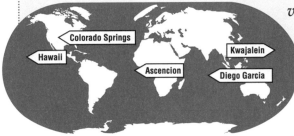

earth every 12 hours. There are also five stations on the ground in Hawaii (Pacific Ocean), Ascension Island (South Atlantic Ocean), Diego Garcia (Indian Ocean), Kwajalein (Western Pacific), and Colorado Springs that monitor these satellites to make sure they're exactly where they're supposed to be at all times.

GPS is used for many, many things beyond its original military application. This system can provide your location to within less than ten feet! And it can give the information to you in a variety of ways, the two most common being coordinates based on latitude and longitude or coordinates based on the Universal Transverse Mercator (UTM) grid.

How does GPS work? The satellites constantly transmit information back to earth by radio signal and a code. Each satellite has an atomic clock that allows it to send the codes at exactly the same time. This accuracy is very important for the functioning of GPS.

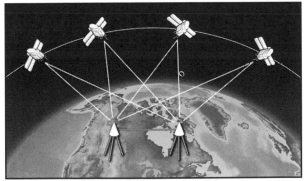

GPS satellites transmitting to ground stations.

UNIVERSAL TRANSVERSE MERCATOR (UTM) GRID

This system was developed to be a simple way to define a coordinate on the earth's surface. Like many navigational tools, UTM has a military background. After World War II, the nations in NATO (the North Atlantic Treaty Organization) agreed that as long as each nation's military used their own coordinate system, it would be impossible to precisely coordinate military movements between nations. The new system became known as the UTM system.

This grid divides the world into 60 north-south zones, each covering a strip 6 degrees wide in longitude. The zones are numbered consecutively beginning with Zone 1, which is between 180 degrees and 174 degrees west longitude, and progressing eastward to Zone 60 where the zones meet at 180 degrees east longitude. Each zone is measured north and east in meters (a meter is 39 inches or just over a yard). The "northing" (adding north) values are measured from the equator. Developers of the grid assigned the number 10,000,000 meters to the equator. Northing numbers larger than 10,000,000 are north of the equator; smaller than 10,000,000 are south of the equator. Each zone is further divided by a central meridian, which is assigned an "easting" (measuring east) value of 500,000 meters. An easting number less than 500,000 will be west of the central meridian in each zone, greater than 500,000 will be east of the central meridian.

Why do we need to know all this? Because almost every aeronautical, nautical, or topographic map you pick up will have the UTM grid overlaid on it. Some grids will just exist as tick marks on the edges of the map—you have to draw the lines yourself—but others will have the grid drawn in. On large-scale maps the UTM grids are 1,000 meters or one kilometer east–west and 1,000 meters or one kilometer north–south. This makes it easy to estimate distance because there's a known distance between the grid lines. Your GPS unit can give you the UTM coordinates for a position, which you can then locate on your map.

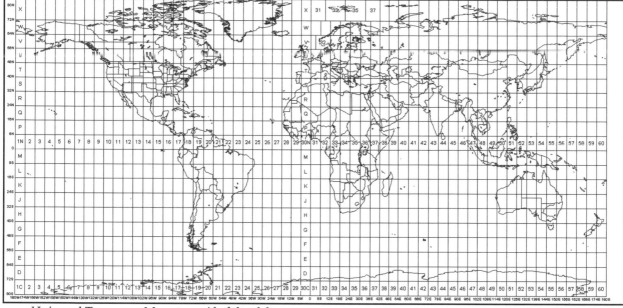

Universal Transverse Mercator grid of the globe.

Use of GPS is free, and the GPS user (this can be just about anyone: a hiker, biker, fisherman, delivery person, etc.) is in control of the receiver. For the hiker, this would be a little handheld unit that runs off two AAA batteries. When the receiver is turned on, it listens to the radio signals and figures out satellite location. It picks the four satellites that are currently overhead and uses the information from these satellites to determine position on the ground.

A whole lot of complicated calculations occur that the user never needs to know about (thank goodness) but basically, the GPS receiver measures the time it takes for the radio signal transmitted from each satellite to travel to the receiver. The distance of the satellite to the receiver can then be calculated by multiplying the travel time by the speed of the radio waves. This is why time is so important to GPS. The signal is traveling at 186,000 miles per second so you need a very, very accurate stopwatch to determine time traveled. This is why there are four satellites used to determine position—three of them are used to triangulate and the fourth is used as a way to correct any discrepancies in the time.

GPS receiver.

NAVIGATION ON MARS

A Mars Rover is a vehicle used to explore the surface of Mars. Since people haven't traveled to Mars yet, all of the Mars Rovers have been robots capable of navigating somewhat independently of NASA control. So far NASA has sent three Rovers to Mars, named Sojourner, Spirit, and Opportunity. A Mars Rover uses something called an integrated autonomous navigation system. The system integrates dead reckoning, inertial navigation, and stereoscopic vision. Using hazard avoidance software, the Rover

Illustration of a Mars Rover.

stops and reassesses its location and the surrounding terrain every 10 seconds. What's the biggest initial obstacle the people working on Mars Rover navigation have to overcome? The lack of magnetic poles, which prevents the use of a magnetic compass. Once you go into space, navigating becomes much more complicated because you can't rely on the basic tools, like the compass used by humans for the past several hundred years.

Determining location by GPS became even more exacting in the late 1990s with the implementation of the Wide Area Augmentation System (WAAS). It works through a series of ground stations that receive GPS signals, transmit corrected information back to another satellite, which then goes to the GPS receiver. WAAS reduces the margin of error and was added to provide increased accuracy for use by commercial airplane navigation systems—this is particularly important during landing. With WAAS, the accuracy increased from being able to pinpoint a position within about 50 feet to within less than 10 feet.

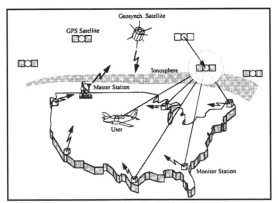

How the WAAS system makes GPS more accurate.

Navigation in Action
How to Find Your Way Using Maps, Compasses, and GPS

So far we have learned about people who have dared to venture beyond the known world. We followed Christopher Columbus, Magellan, and Captain Cook across vast and uncharted seas. They left the comfort of their homes because they had a quest for knowledge (of course, the prospect of finding a water route to China and becoming fabulously wealthy didn't hurt either). We've traveled across Arctic waters with a Viking and an early Ice Age navigator, and even traversed potentially dangerous lands with Marco Polo and the Lewis and Clark expedition. Now it's time to get out of our chairs and begin to explore the world around us.

Columbus

Magellan

Cook

Learn how to read a road map and what all those symbols mean

See the difference between varying scales on a map

Decipher a topographic map and see what the different contour lines mean

Use a compass

Try geocaching

But how do we do that?

First we need to learn more how to read maps. Let's concentrate on land maps first. There are a couple of different kinds of maps that you're likely to come across: road maps (also known as planimetric maps), and topographic maps. Both give a wealth of information if you know how to read them.

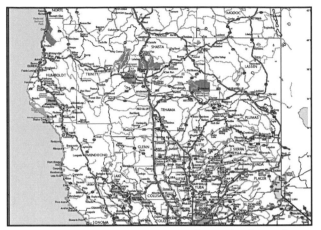

Example of a road map.

All maps share a couple of things. First, look for the scale, usually indicated along the bottom of the map. The scale tells you how many centimeters or inches on the map equal kilometers or miles in real life.

Most road maps are printed on the same size sheet of paper so they can be folded the same way and all fit neatly

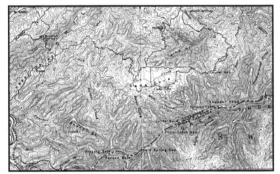

Example of a topographic map.

into the glove compartment of a car. That means, if they're maps of single states, the scale will vary because the state will be drawn to fit the standard-size paper. For example, since New Jersey is a much smaller state than New York, the scale may differ so that 1 inch equals 5 miles in New Jersey and 1 inch equals 11 miles in New York.

Second, all maps should indicate which direction is north. By convention, north is oriented at the top of the map, but always make sure to look for an

WORDS TO KNOW

planimetric map: *shows the horizontal position features. Sometimes called a line map.*

topographic map: *represents both horizontal and vertical features, either with contour lines or spot elevations. Also called contour maps.*

contour lines: *curves that connect continuous points of the same altitude.*

arrow with north written by it that points in the direction north. Often, on a topographic map, there will be one arrow pointing to geographic north, then another arrow pointing to magnetic north, with the angle and direction of declination written in.

Road Maps

Let's walk through the details found on a road map.

First, look for a box on your map that is titled Legend. The legend box will tell you some cool things about the map. At the top of the box it will say who published the map and in what year—this can be helpful if you want the most up-to-date information and you see the year is 1975! Things change, including roads.

Example of a map legend.

Inside the legend box you'll get the keys to reading the map. Along the bottom of the box will be the scale. You can read distance in terms of inch per miles or per kilometers.

On a New York State road map published by AAA in 2002, the legend shows that a yellow line is a toll highway (meaning you have to pay), a fat dark-red line is a divided highway, a thinner dark-red line is a two- or three-lane road, an even thinner light-red line is a paved two-lane road, a line that alternates between red and pink sections is a gravel road, and two thin, black parallel lines designate a dirt road.

Cities are areas shaded yellow. Towns are circles. The state capital is a black star enclosed in a black circle. The county seat is a black dot enclosed in a black circle. County route numbers are in black squares. State routes are in red ovals. U.S. routes are in red shields. Interstate highways are blue shields with the numbers written in white. We can also see that

Map of Georgia showing county lines.

What is the difference between a planimetric map and a topograhic map?

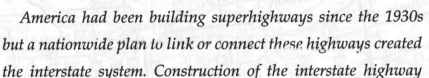

THE INTERSTATE HIGHWAY SYSTEM

Nearly every interstate highway is a controlled-access superhighway or freeway, meaning that you can't just get on it anywhere—there are certain entry and exit points. The interstate system was authorized during the presidency of President Dwight D. Eisenhower. He had crossed the country as a young soldier, and he was also impressed by the German autobahn network during his military service.

President Dwight D. Eisenhower

America had been building superhighways since the 1930s but a nationwide plan to link or connect these highways created the interstate system. Construction of the interstate highway system lasted for 35 years and cost $114 billion. As of 2004, the system contains over 42,700 miles of roads.

The numbering scheme for the highway system is administered by the American Association of State Highway and Transportation Officials and is pretty cool. The major highways are given one- or two-digit route numbers. Even-numbered highways go generally east-west, and odd-numbered highways go generally north-south. Odd-numbered routes increase from west to east; and even numbered routes increase from south to north. Numbers divisible by five are roads that go all the way (or nearly all the way) across the country from one border of the United States to another. For example, I-5 runs 1,381 miles from Blaine, Washington, near the Canadian border to a few miles south of San Diego at the Mexican border. I-95 runs 1,921 miles from Miami to Canada along the east coast through New England. In addition, I-10 runs from Los Angeles, California, to Jacksonville, Florida, while I-80 runs from San Francisco to Fort Lee, New Jersey. There is also an I-90 that runs from Seattle to Boston, and shares a portion of its routing with I-80.

Map of New Hampshire—distance from arrow labeled "A" to arrow labeled "B" is 6 miles; from "A" to "C" is 23 miles.

campgrounds are designated by a little teepee and ski areas show a little red skier shaded in yellow.

Parks are shaded in green. Military areas are shaded brown. Bodies of water like lakes, rivers, ponds, and oceans are colored blue. The name of the body of water is written either in the water (look at a lake) or alongside it (look at a stream).

Now look closely at your road map. Blue, dashed lines delineate counties and the county names are written in blue on the map. If you follow a road—any road—you'll see little, tiny arrows. Find one arrow then follow the road further on and you'll find another. Between the two arrows is a tiny number written in red or black. This is the number of miles between those two points.

Somewhere near the center of your road map is a stylized compass rose showing north, which should point toward the top of your map.

Just by taking a quick glance at the map you can take in a lot of information. First, if you want to travel across the state—east to west—you can see what roads are available, and can make a decision whether to drive on a main highway or a back road. This will determine how quickly you arrive at your destination. Back roads tend to be slower because they're only two lanes and they usually go through towns, meaning you'll be slowing down to go the town speed limit and maybe stopping at lights and stop signs. Sometimes you might like to drive the secondary (or back roads) in order to see the towns and eat in local restaurants. These are the kinds of decisions the driver has to make.

planimetric . . . from the Latin planum, *which means "flat ground" and* metria, *"measurement"*

123

What sections of the country does Interstate 75 connect? Can you guess?

ACTIVITY

Using a Road Map

This activity will reinforce some of your map-reading skills and teach you how to plot a course.

Supplies:

- **Road map with your home town on it**
- **Piece of paper and pencil**

Instructions:

- Find your hometown on the map.

- Pick a destination about six inches from your town.

- Look at the scale of your map.

- Fold your piece of paper in half and put it on the map so it goes through your town and the destination. Put tick marks on the paper at both places and measure this distance against the scale to get an idea of how far you have to travel.

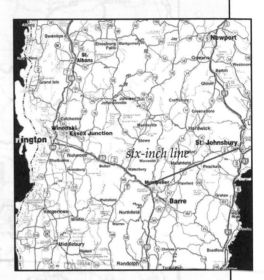

six-inch line

- Look at your map and plot your course—decide which roads you'll take to get to your destination. Plot the straightest course possible.

- Add up the little tiny numbers on your map to get a true distance to your destination—almost every map has these tiny numbers that represent the distance between little points or arrows placed on each road.

- Compare your "as the crow flies" number to actual distance determined by adding up the numbers.

The next time you're on a road trip with your parents, offer to be the navigator. Then use a road map and tell them the routes to take (make sure to note the direction, i.e., Route 81 north) and which direction to turn to get to these routes.

Map of Manhattan.

Sometimes you might see a lot of roads going in more or less the same direction, say southwest to northeast, and few roads running perpendicular to them. Why would that be? You also notice the streams and rivers running in the same general direction. One thing road maps don't show you are hills or mountains, but you can infer from the road patterns that there is some kind of obstacle that determined how the roads would be built. This is why road maps are called planimetric maps.

Now turn your road map over. The other side will show some part of the state in greater detail. For example, if you have a New York State map, the flip side will show Manhattan and Long Island in greater detail. Check the legend box and notice that the scale has changed. Instead of being 1 inch to 11 miles, the scale might go down to 1 inch equalling 5.25 miles. That certainly makes a difference as you're figuring out driving time.

This side of the road map also includes an outline of the state with straight black lines connecting the major cities. On one side of the lines are numbers written in red—this is the distance between two points—and on the other side of the lines are numbers written in blue—this is the average time it takes a driver to go this distance.

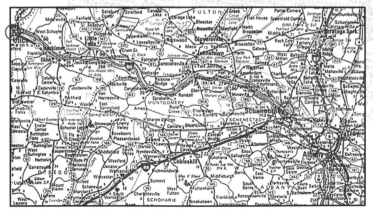

Schenectady to Utica.

For example, on the New York map, it's 75 miles from Utica to Schenectady and it should take one hour, nine minutes (1:09) to drive that distance. Going to the west, it's 74 miles from Batavia to Wellsville and the estimated driving time is one hour and 49 minutes (1:49). Why the big difference to cover the same distance? Turn over the map and notice that you can travel on a main interstate between Utica and Schenectady. However, going from Batavia to Wellsville will mean taking a state highway, then an interstate, then another interstate, and finally a secondary road to reach the destination.

The flip side of the road map also includes an index or an alphabetical listing of all the place names on the map. Find your town, then notice that there's a letter-number combination following it. Look along the left or right edge of your map and notice that the alphabet runs along the edge, each letter separated by an arrow. Now look along the top or bottom of the map and notice consecutive numbers separated by arrows. Think of your map being laid out like a big grid. To locate Derry, New Hampshire, find the letter M then run your finger across the map from the M until it intersects with the number 8. Derry should be within the inch square right about where your finger stopped. Pretty cool.

How do you know if the town you look up on the index will be on the main side of the map or the flip side? Notice that although the alphabet letters on the flip side stay the same, the numbers along the top and bottom are higher. If the index said that Derry was at

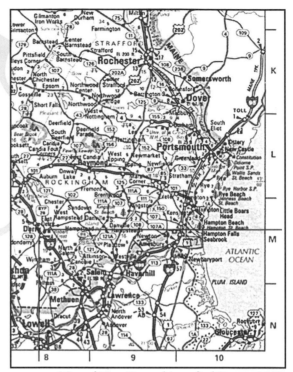

Map of New Hampshire—find Derry at M8.

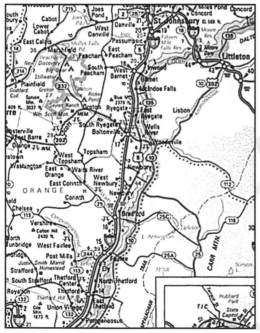

I-91 runs north–south in Vermont along the Connecticut River.

Why do maps come in varying scales?

M-12, you would know to look on the flip side because the numbers along that side run from 11 up.

You can also locate parks, forests, military facilities, Indian reservations, lakes and reservoirs, and airports by using the index.

Road maps are neat and the more you look at them and understand them, the more information you'll be able to see. You'll notice that towns and large highways tend to be situated along rivers. You'll get a feel for direction and what lies north, south, east, or west of your town. And you'll get a general sense of distance.

If you find yourself going on a driving trip with your parents, take out the road map for your area. Ask your mother or father where you are right now and then locate that position on the map. Now look for where you started from and then look for your destination (the ending point). Locate all of these on the map and ask your mother or father what route/road they're planning to take. Follow along by noticing towns you pass. Notice if the road follows a stream or river. Look for geographic or man-made features that might show up on your road map (for example, lakes, rivers, airports, parks, and military installations). Also look for intersections—places where one route crosses another—to check whether you're right or not.

Now try to figure out which way your car is going to have to turn when you go from one route to another. Here's a hint. If you orient, or hold, the map in the direction you're traveling, sometimes it's easier to figure out which direction to turn. As you get better at reading maps, you'll be able to figure out direction without holding the map upside down or sideways.

Topographic Maps

Now that you know how to read and find your way along man-made roads, what other kinds of maps are out there? We've already looked at a modern road map, but there are other kinds of maps out there. In this section we'll take a look at topographic maps and learn how to read their symbols. Then we'll learn how

Topographic comes from the Greek topo, *which means "place" and* graphein . . . *"to write."*

127

to use a basic orienteering compass. The great part about learning how to read a map and use a modern compass is that once you learn and master these skills, they stick! With a topographic map and compass you can find your way around anywhere in the world.

Topographic maps are available for most of the United States and Canada, and are prepared by the United States Geological Survey (USGS). Symbols used on these topographic maps are similar to map symbols used around the world, so if you can read a USGS map, chances are you can read a map from any other country.

Maps are drawn to specific scales. The scale lets you, the map reader, know the distance between two points, as well as the area covered by the map. Three common scales for USGS maps are 1 unit to 250,000 units (1:250,000), 1 unit to 62,500 units (1:62,500), and 1 unit to 24,000 units (1:24,000). A unit of measurement used on the USGS map is 1 inch. One inch measured on a USGS topographic map represents so many inches in the field. There are also variations on these common scales like 1:63,360 or 1:100,000.

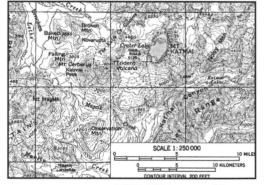

1:250,000 topographic map.

1:250,000 maps—The scale of 1 inch to 250,000 inches means that 1 inch on the map equals 4 miles in real life. Actually 253,440 inches equals 4 miles but that's a messy number to try to work with so it was rounded off for simplicity's sake.

These maps cover an area of 6,346 to 8,669 square miles (depending on latitude). This is the kind of topographic map you'd use if you wanted to get a general idea of the geographic features of an area. It would help you plan your trip or hiking expedition by helping you figure out points of interest within a distance of about 100 miles.

1:62,500 topographic map.

1:62,500 maps—In this map 1 inch equals 1 mile. These maps cover a range from 195 square miles in the north to 271 square miles in the south, closer to the equator. Can you think why these maps cover more area in the south? Think about flat maps and Mercator projections and remember that as you travel further north, the area gets stretched out on a map because you're spreading the meridians—lines of longitude—apart to keep them perpendicular to the parallels, or lines of latitude.) These maps are very helpful for hiking because they contain enough detail to really tell you about the terrain.

1:24,000 maps—On these maps, 1 inch equals 2,000 feet. They cover an area ranging from 49 square miles along the Canadian border to 68 square miles in

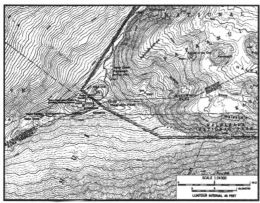

1:24,000 topographic map.

southern Florida. These maps show the most detail and are terrific if you're trying to find your way in a limited area with a radius of about 4 miles.

The USGS has divided each state into rectangles—what they call "quadrangles." A quadrangle measures 7.5 minutes of latitude by 7.5 minutes of longitude and is designated by the name of the town or some natural feature found within the area.

You can request a Topographic Map Index Circular of the state you're interested in and a booklet about topographic maps from the USGS.

Reading Your Topographic Map

In order to read your map, break it down into the five Ds—description, details, directions, distances, and designations.

Description—The description of your map is found in its margin, so let's take a trip around the edge of the map.

First, the name of your map area is found along the top (north edge) of your map. This name is repeated at the bottom with the number of the map. You'll also find names in parentheses on each edge–these are the names of the maps immediately adjacent. So if you're planning a hike or a trip that extends off the map, you know the next map you need to look for.

Your map also tells you where you are in the world by giving you your longitude and latitude numbers. As we know, the lines of longitude (or meridian lines) run north–south, whereas the lines of latitude (parallels) run east–west.

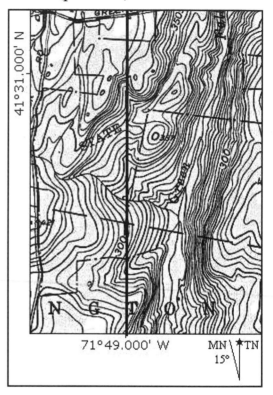

You'll find tiny numbers in the margins that look something like 73°22'30" that you would read as "73 degrees, 22 minutes, 30 seconds." If you remember, we've learned that 1 degree equals 60 nautical miles or 69 land miles. There are 60 minutes in a degree so 1 minute equals 6,080 feet, and there are 60 seconds in a minute so one second equals about 101 feet.

Along the bottom, or south edge, of your map are some dates. It might read something like "Aerial photographs taken 1948. Field check 1952–53," and then to the right there might be a single date like "1953." This would tell you that the map you're looking at was developed from aerial photos one year, then checked by surveyors in subsequent years (1952–53 in our example). Then the single date is the edition of your map.

Why is this stuff important? Well, if your map covers an area with a town in it, there could be a lot more houses added to the town in the past half-century. Also, natural features could change. A dam could have been built across the river that shows up in your map, creating a lake. A swamp could have been drained. A new road could have been built. You shouldn't worry about these things before you go out into the field, but you should be aware that things do change.

Details—The details on your topographic map include man-made, water, vegetation, and elevation features. All of these have symbols associated with them and you have to be able to remember what these symbols stand for. Luckily, whoever

What do the quadrangles of the USGS maps represent? How many miles by how many miles?

HOW TO READ A TOPOGRAPHIC MAP

Here's one way to start to try and understand contour lines. Imagine taking a cone and dipping it   large end first—into a pail of water so that one inch of the cone is submerged. Take the cone out, draw a line with a marker where the watermark ends. You should have a circle going around the cone. Dip the cone in so that it's submerged an inch beyond the first watermark. Take the cone out and draw another line where the second watermark ends. You should have two lines an inch apart, encircling the cone. Do this several more times, putting the cone in an inch further each time. Now look at the cone from above. What do you see? You should see several concentric circles. If you saw concentric circles on a topographic map, you would know you're looking at a cone-shaped feature.

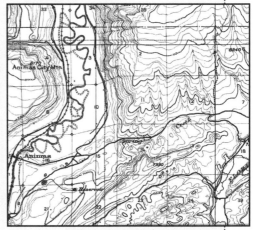

This sounds more complicated than it really is, but reading contour lines does take practice. There are some general rules you can follow, however, which should make it easier to envision what you see on the map as three-dimensional objects.

If adjacent contour lines are spaced far apart and are fairly evenly spaced, then you're looking at a broad, gentle slope. When lines are close together, then you're looking at a hill—the closer the lines are, the steeper the slope, until they're right on top of one another, which would indicate a cliff.

If your topographic map is of a hilly or mountainous area, you'll notice that a number of contour lines may make a V shape. Where contour lines cross a river or stream, they make a V with the point of the V pointing uphill. You may also notice contour lines that are U-shaped. If the U points downhill, it's a spur on a hill or mountain. If the U points slightly uphill, you're looking at a broad, glacial valley.

Name the four types of topographic map symbols and their corresponding colors.

ACTIVITY

Match Contour Maps to Hill Profiles

This exercise will help you to become more familiar with how a two-dimensional map can translate to a three-dimensional topographic figure. (Hint: lines that are close together represent steep slopes.)

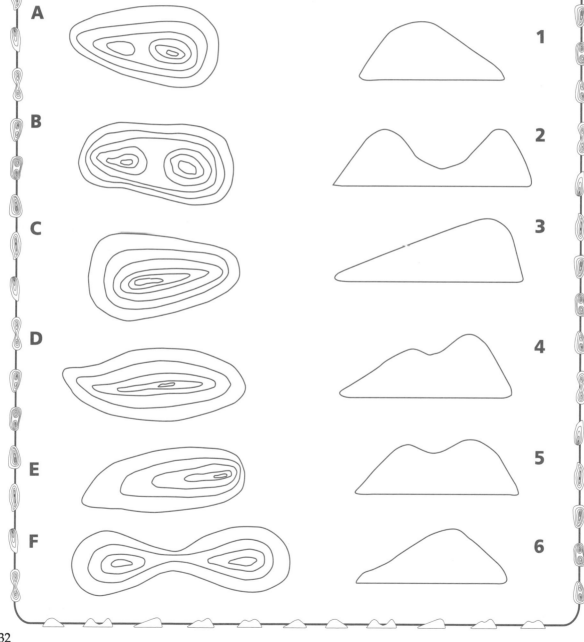

ACTIVITY

Understanding Contour Lines

In this activity you'll make a cross-section or a profile of a contour map. The goal is to eventually be able to look at a topographic map and see not just squiggly lines, but the shapes of the features the contour lines represent.

Supplies:

• Piece of graph paper

• Pencil

• Ruler

Instructions:

• Transfer the points designated by the letters from the map below to your graph paper. The scale along the bottom edge of your graph should be the same as that on the map below. Make every two or three horizontal lines on your graph paper equal to 20 feet for your vertical scale. This map represents an island, so points A and J are at sea level (0 feet).

• After creating your profile, answer the following question: If you were hiking on this island, which side would you choose to climb in order to reach the summit?

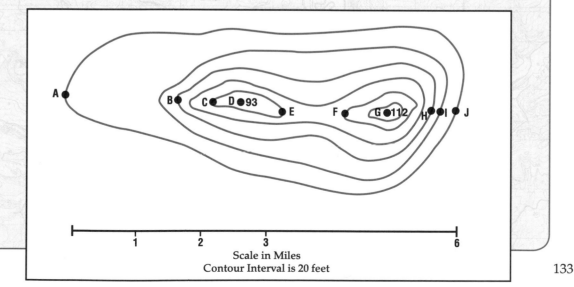

Scale in Miles
Contour Interval is 20 feet

came up with the symbols made them look like tiny pictograms of what they're portraying, for example, a church shows up as a tiny circle with a cross on top.

Each of the four types of map symbols has its own distinctive color: man-made features are black; water features are blue; vegetation features are green; and elevation features are brown. Man-made features include roads and trails, houses, buildings, railroads, power lines, dams, and bridges.

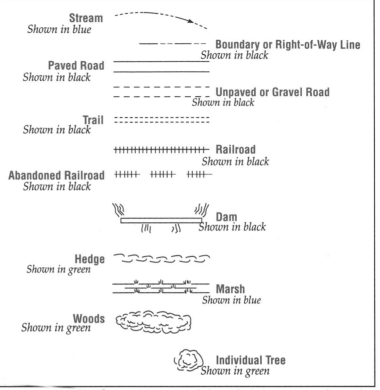

Some samples of contour map symbols with their corresponding color.

Water includes rivers, canals, lakes, oceans, swamps, and marshes. Typical vegetation features include woods and orchards.

Being able to figure out the elevation features, marked by brown contour lines, are why most people use topographic maps. When you first look at a topographic map, it just looks like a mess of brown lines, but the placement of these lines gives you an enormous amount of information.

A contour line is an imaginary line on the ground where every point on that line is at the same height above sea level. The distance between each contour line is called a contour interval and can vary from map to map depending on how hilly or level the land is. The contour interval will always be written along the bottom border of your map. It will say something like "CONTOUR INTERVAL 20 FEET."

Every fifth contour line will be a bolder, heavier line and is called an index contour line. A number written on the line—something like 800—indicates that

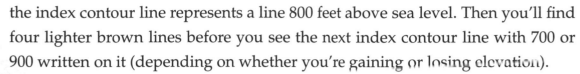

the index contour line represents a line 800 feet above sea level. Then you'll find four lighter brown lines before you see the next index contour line with 700 or 900 written on it (depending on whether you're gaining or losing elevation).

Often, you'll see precise elevation numbers next to mountain peaks, road intersections, or lakes. These indicate the elevation of the feature given to the nearest foot.

The key to interpreting contours is to be able to visualize them in three dimensions. Try to see more than just a bunch of squiggly brown lines to get a sense of the overall topography of the area. First, look for low spots by looking for contour lines with the lowest numbers (closest to sea level). Follow one index contour line around the map and note where it goes. Contour lines don't ever cross each other. They can be on top of each other (as in a sheer cliff) but they cannot cross. So look for the next index contour line, read the number, and then you'll

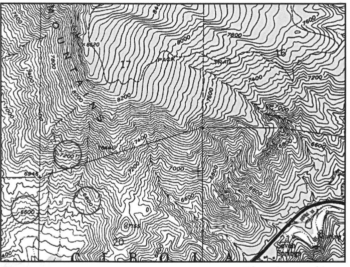

Elevation markings.

know whether you're going up in elevation or down. Start noticing the **V**s for the streams. Contour lines that form closed shapes indicate that you're coming to the top (or the bottom) of some geographic feature such as a peak of a mountain.

Practice, practice, practice.

Directions—As with most maps, on contour maps north is oriented at the top, south is at the bottom, west is left, and east is right. If you look at the bottom of your topographic map you'll find a little diagram with an elongated triangle in it. One leg of the triangle will be marked "true north," the other will be marked "magnetic north," and there will be a degree written between the two. This diagram is labeled "Approximate Mean Declination." Don't worry about this right now. We've already learned that there's a difference between true north and magnetic north. USGS has gone to the trouble of letting us know what the declination, or deviation, is for that particular quadrangle so that we can set our compasses properly.

You want to be able to draw a line from point A to point B on your map (where you want to begin and where you want to end), then have that line correspond to a compass direction. Why? So that when you're actually in the field with a map in one hand and compass in the other, you'll be able to figure out which direction to walk.

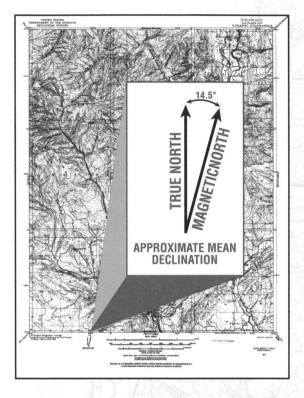

Distances—Remember when you looked at the information found in the margin of your topographic map? One of the pieces of information you discovered was the scale, written as 1:250,000, 1:62,500, or 1:24,000. Remember that this tells you how many inches in the field correspond to one inch on the map. For example, if it is 3.5 inches from point A to point B and the scale is 1:62,500 (1 inch equals 1 mile) then we know that the distance between point A and point B equals three and one half miles.

Another way to measure distance is to use the map's bar scale. You'll find it along the bottom edge of your map and it will be calibrated in miles, feet, yards, meters, or kilometers. Draw a line from point A to point B on your map, then measure the length of the line with the ruler and compute the distance. Another way to determine the distance is to take the edge of a piece of paper and mark off where point A is and where point B is on the paper's edge. Then hold the paper to the bar scale and figure out the distance.

Why should we care about the distance from point A to point B? For one thing,

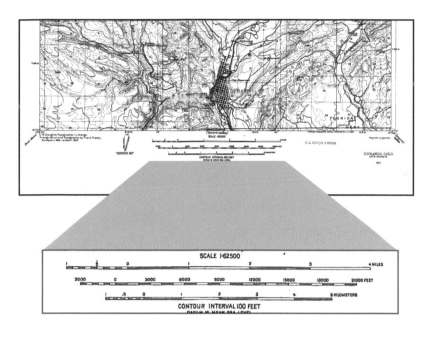

it's nice to know how far you're going to walk before you set out on your hike. Depending on the topography of the area—whether you have to walk up some hills and through some gorges or if the terrain is fairly flat—you should be able to figure out how long it might take you to cover the distance.

You should figure out the number of minutes it takes you to cover one mile under different circumstances: road, field, woods, and mountains. You should also know the number of paces it takes you to cover a certain distance (you count a pace as every two steps or by always counting every time your right foot hits the ground). This gives you two different ways to estimate distance out in the field—either by how much time has passed since you started walking or by counting paces.

Designations—Suppose you're hiking and want to meet up with a friend at point B. When describing where point B is, you'd look for the nearest place-name designation, for example, the name of a mountain, lake, stream, boundary line, or town.

If point B is not near someplace with a place name designation, find the nearest word printed on your map and describe point B's position in reference to that. Let's say point B is a mile and a half from Huckleberry Mountain. You would tell your friend something like the following: 1½ inches southwest of the H in Huckleberry Mountain, and your friend would be able to locate point B.

Remember that you and your friend need to be using the same edition of the topographic map or else you could get confused—place names could have changed or disappeared altogether, or be printed differently on the map.

How to Use an Orienteering Compass

We've learned about the origins of the magnetic compass and how this little instrument—small enough to fit in the palm of your hand—changed our view of the world by opening up the seas and unknown lands to exploration. Now we're going to learn how to use a compass and embark on our own explorations.

A modern orienteering compass sits on a clear plastic rectangular base plate that's calibrated on its sides with scales that correspond to those found on topographic maps. For example, you can use an orienteering compass as a ruler to measure distance on maps with one side for maps scaled at 1:24,000 and the other for 1:62,500. One edge is in inches. There's also an arrow from the actual compass to the opposite edge of the base plate. That's the direction-of-travel arrow.

The compass itself consists of a magnetic compass needle with one end painted red that always points to magnetic north. On the plastic underneath the magnetic compass needle is another red arrow called an orienteering arrow and a series of black, parallel lines called orienteering lines. You line up your compass needle with the orienteering arrow by moving the black compass dial that surrounds the compass needle. Rotate the dial until the needle is inside the orienteering arrow. You have found north. Magnetic north, to be precise.

Now notice that the outer ring of the black compass dial (called the compass housing) is calibrated from 0 to 360. These are the

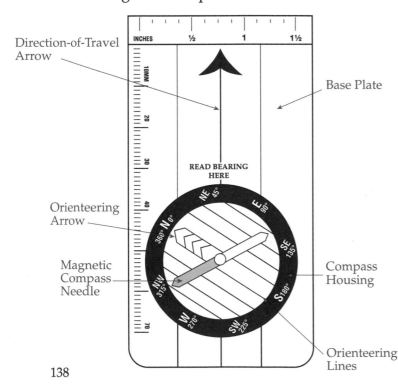

Direction-of-Travel Arrow

Base Plate

Orienteering Arrow

Magnetic Compass Needle

READ BEARING HERE

Compass Housing

Orienteering Lines

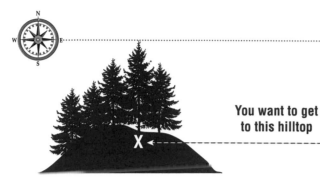

You want to get to this hilltop

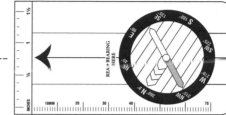

Turn compass housing

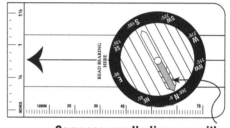

Compass needle lines up with orienteering arrow

number of degrees in a circle. The inner ring has eight cardinal points notated (N, NE, E, etc.), or the cardinal points may be on the ring with the degree markings.

How do you find direction with an orienteering compass? Hold the compass at about waist level. Now point the direction-of-travel arrow toward a prominent object in the landscape (like a big tree or some rocks on a distant hill). Turn the compass housing so that the red compass needle is over the orienteering arrow on the base plate. This will properly orient your compass. Now read the number off the compass housing—this is called your bearing.

Following a bearing with an orienteering compass is easy. Suppose you want to walk to a distant hilltop. Hold your compass at waist level and point the direction-of-travel arrow toward the hilltop. Move the compass housing so that the compass needle is over the orienteering arrow on the base plate. Note the compass bearing. Start walking in the direction of the hill. DO NOT MOVE THE COMPASS HOUSING ONCE YOU BEGIN TO WALK.

You are able to stay on course by checking that you're still oriented in the right direction. Frequently check your bearing by stopping and holding your compass at waist height and making sure that the compass needle and orienteering arrow are lined up. Do this by turning your whole body to align the compass needle with the orienteering arrow. Note your bearing. Then walk in the direction of

ACTIVITY

Traveling by Compass

This activity will test your skill with a compass.

Supplies:
- One quarter
- An orienteering compass

Instructions:
- Go out into a flat field.
- Place a quarter on the ground at your feet.
- Choose a number between 0 degrees and 120 degrees.
- Set your compass by turning the compass housing until your number is at the direction-of-travel arrow (i.e., 45 degrees).
- Line up your magnetic compass needle with the north orienteering arrow by holding your compass at waist level in front of you and slowly turning your body.
- Look up and find a landmark in the direction you've chosen and walk toward it for 20 paces, which should be around 100 feet, then stop.
- Look at your compass and add 120° to your original number. Move your compass housing to register the new number. Hold your compass in front of you and slowly turn your body until the arrows align.
- Look up and find a landmark in the new direction and walk toward it for 20 paces, then stop.
- Do this a third time, then stop and look down. Is your quarter at your feet?

You've just walked the three legs of an equilateral triangle.

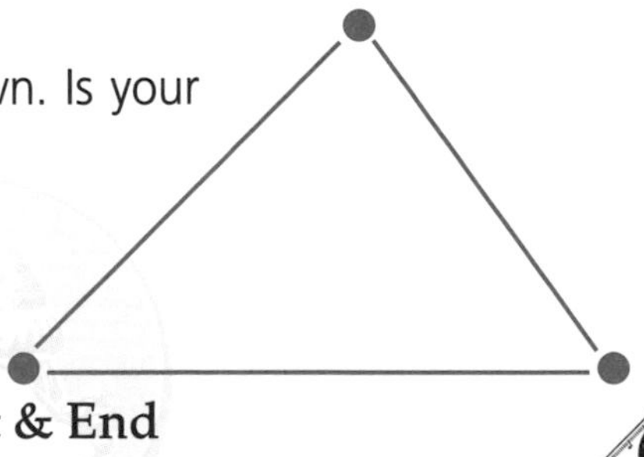

Start & End

your direction-of-travel arrow. If you lose sight of the hilltop, don't worry. Line up your red arrows, find an object in front of you that lies on that bearing, then walk toward it. Do this repeatedly until you see your hilltop again. Remember not to move the housing dial.

When you want to travel back to your original location, do not move your compass housing to take another bearing (you probably won't even be able to see your original starting place). Rather, turn the base plate of the compass around so that the direction-of-travel arrow points toward you. Then turn your whole body until the north arrows line up. Then walk *against* the direction-of-travel arrow, taking frequent sightings to keep your compass orientation in line with your destination. DO NOT MOVE THE COMPASS HOUSING while you're making your way back to where you started.

Remember from our earlier discussion on the development of the compass that there are actually two norths. Your compass always points to magnetic north, which is not the same as geographic north. Maps are drawn using geographic or true north. At the bottom of any topographic map is the declination, or the angle between magnetic and true north, which will vary depending on where you are. Most orienteering compasses have a way to manually correct your compass for this angle. Some compasses have a tiny key attached to the neck cord. This key turns a little screw on the back of the compass that will shift the compass housing to the correct declination and this will line up the orienteering lines with the declination. This is the easiest way to deal with the difference between true and magnetic north. You must, however, remember to reset your declination for every topographic map you use; otherwise, you can be way off in your course plotting.

Another way to deal with declination is to add or subtract the number of degrees shown on the map and then turn the compass housing that many degrees before you begin any map reading. If the declination is west, add the number of degrees (remember, "west is best" best meaning something has been added). If the declination is east, subtract the number of degrees (remember, "east is least").

West is best = add
East is least = subtract

Another way is to draw lines directly onto your map that line up with the declination. Look at the little arrow on the bottom of the map that shows true north and magnetic north and then draw lines across your map that line up with magnetic north. Now when you put your compass on top of the map with the lines drawn on them, you line up the orienteering lines with those drawn lines.

Although there are several different kinds of compasses, use an orienteering compass for a couple of reasons. First, these compasses are fairly inexpensive (under 10 dollars). Second, an orienteering compass is easy to use, particularly in combination with topographic maps. The calibrated rulers on the sides of the base plate are wonderful because they allow you to compute distances between points easily.

These compasses were developed for orienteering competitions, or races. Originally a navigational and map-reading exercise used by the Swedish army in the early part of the twentieth century,

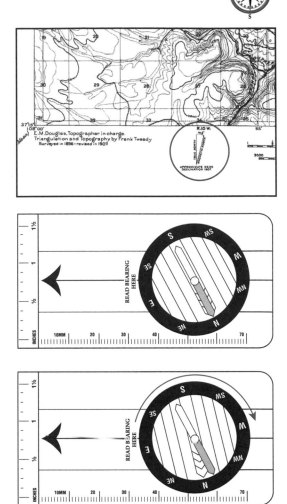

Using the map above, the declination is 14.5°E. Therefore, you will "subtract" 14.5 degrees using the rotating compass housing on your orienteering compass.

orienteering has grown into a global sport. An orienteering race can be an activity for people of all different skill levels of navigating. There are several different kinds of orienteering races but they all involve using topographic maps, compasses, and control points (these are numbered stations along the course where you

Calculating bearings at an orienteeering competition.

punch or stamp a card that you carry with you). In the highly competitive cross-country orienteering races, it takes quick thinking, excellent map-reading and compass-reading skills, as well as athletic ability to do well.

Using a map and compass together, which is the basis of orienteering and off-trail hiking, is really fun once you get the hang of it. First you have to orient your map with your compass. Set your compass so that the orienteering arrow and 360-degree mark are aligned. Now lay your compass on your map and turn the map until your compass points to north.

Find your beginning point and your first destination. Set the straightedge of your compass along the line between the two points. Your compass needle will still be pointing to north (it always does), but don't worry about that. Draw a line between the two points. Now turn the compass housing so that the black orienteering lines underneath the compass needle lie parallel to a meridian line (a north-south line) on your map. Read the degree that's on the compass housing at the direction-of-travel arrow (which is parallel to the straightedge between the two points). This is your first bearing. Let's say it's 224 degrees. Write "224°" on the line. You can repeat this for your other destination points.

When you get to your start point in the field, set your compass to your first bearing by turning the compass housing until 224 degrees is aligned with the direction-of-travel arrow. Hold your compass in your hand at waist level with the direction-of-travel arrow facing out. Now turn your entire body until the red compass needle is lined up with the orienteering arrow beneath it. Pick a landmark—something like a tree, rock, or bush—in front of you and walk toward it. When you reach your landmark take another sighting with your compass and choose another landmark that lines up with 224 degrees. Continue this until you reach your destination.

Make sure you measure the distance between the points on your map. Either use the straightedge

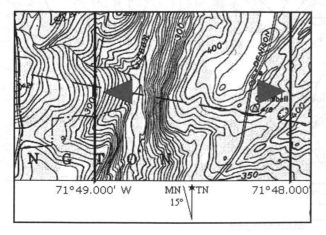

Meridian lines.

ACTIVITY

Working with a Topographic Map

Plot a course of travel using the map to the right. Pretend you have to punch a card at each of the four checkpoints, so accuracy counts. Remember to orient your compass before you start.

Supplies:

- Orienteering compass
- Ruler
- Pencil

Instructions:

Checkpoint 1: find the T in the road ½ inch NE of the "d" in Tompkins-Cortland Community College.

Checkpoint 2: 2⅞ inches NE to the cemetery.

Checkpoint 3: 3 inches NW to the road junction of Malloryville Road and the road that Ts into it south of Beaver Pond.

Checkpoint 4: 2¼ inches SW to road junction of Dutcher and North Roads. Then head back to the beginning spot, which is 4 inches SE from checkpoint 4.

- Figure out the compass bearing for each leg of your journey. Your first bearing should be around 42 degrees.

- Figure out how many feet you have to travel on each leg. Remember that the scale is 1:24,000 so 1 inch equals 2,000 feet. Convert your answer to miles (remember, 5,280 feet equals 1 mile).

- When you look at your beelines (the most direct route) to each checkpoint, do you see a better way to travel? Try to imagine the topography and then make it work for you. Sometimes it makes more sense to traverse the sides of hills along one contour rather than dipping in and out of gullies. Sometimes it also makes more sense to travel along roads or to follow creeks.

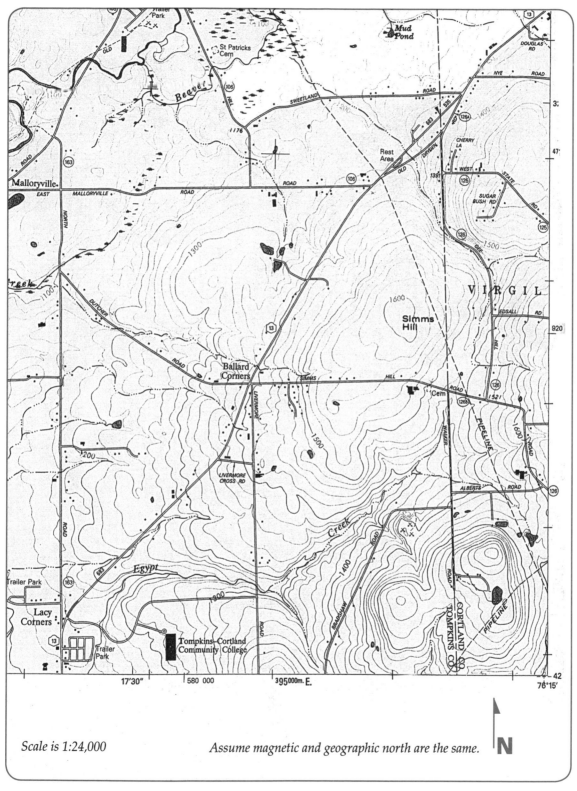

Scale is 1:24,000

Assume magnetic and geographic north are the same.

N

How many feet are in a mile?

that already conforms to the scale of your map, or measure the distance and then convert it to the scale. This will let you know how far you have to walk—a pretty important detail when you're in the field.

There are other ways to use your compass. Say you have been hiking along, but you don't know exactly where you are relative to the map. Look for a landmark—a bend in the river, a distinctively tall peak, or a building like a church. You can take a bearing on the landmark and transfer that information to your map. From where you're standing, hold the compass at waist level, pointing the direction-of-travel arrow toward the landmark. Now turn the compass housing until the two north arrows (the compass needle and the orienteering arrow) coincide. Read the bearing.

Place the direction-of-travel arrow on the landmark on the map and then orient the map toward north making sure the north arrows coincide. Make sure the black orienteering lines beneath the compass needle are parallel to the meridian lines on the map. Slide your compass so you can draw a line using your straightedge, which is parallel

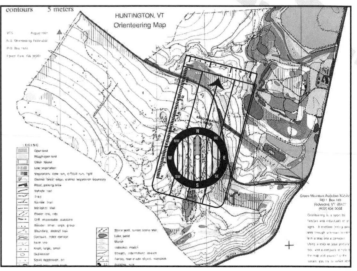

to the direction-of-travel arrow. You are standing somewhere on that line.

If you want to know exactly where you are on that line, you can triangulate, or find your position on the map by taking a bearing off another landmark, and repeat the process in the above paragraph. When you draw the second line on the map, it should cross the first one. Where it crosses should be pretty close to where you're standing.

Using GPS

A handheld GPS receiver can be very helpful with three basic tasks. First, information from your GPS can help lead you to a destination on a map (a paper

146

ACTIVITY

Go on a Treasure Hunt

This is a group activity although two can make it work just fine. This activity needs to be done in two steps.

Supplies:

- Directional compasses
- Small notebook
- Pencil
- 8 to 10 small objects for treasures

Instructions:

- One group or person is responsible for determining the course and placing the treasures and the other group or person follows the directions and retrieves the treasures. Both groups can hide treasures and make maps in separate areas and then switch treasure maps and find the other group's treasures.

- Decide how much territory you want to cover. Make it reasonable. Maybe just use your backyard or a couple of hundred yards around your house.

- Choose a starting place, then determine the direction you're going to head by consulting your compass. Walk to your first destination. Count your paces. When you get there, write "Destination 1" in your notebook and note the compass bearing and the number of paces (remember: a pace is determined by counting every right or left footfall). Put a small object in plain sight at the destination, something like a colorful small toy (a yoyo, for example, or a plastic egg filled with jellybeans) and note what the object is in your notebook.

- Repeat this step until you have 8 to 10 destinations noted in your notebook. Your last destination and your starting place should be the same.

- The second group then takes the notebook and a compass and tries to find all of the objects on the treasure hunt by setting each course and counting paces.

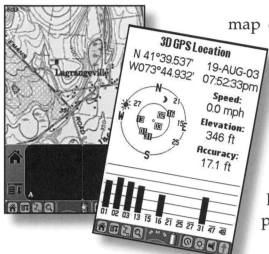

map or an electronic map built into the receiver or downloaded from your computer). Second, a GPS receiver can determine your current position by providing you with either latitude and longitude coordinates or UTM coordinates. You can then locate your position on a map. And third, you can program your GPS to remember your current position so you can return to it later.

As a navigational tool, the GPS receiver can give you a lot of information including distance between points, your speed, a desired course, your current course, and travel time. It can even calculate your estimated time of arrival as well as how much time you've spent hiking. It will also keep track of where you've been, which is enormously helpful for search and rescue units.

A coordinate on a GPS receiver is called a waypoint or a landmark. Your receiver can store hundreds of waypoints in its memory, which can then be retrieved when you need them. You might create a dozen waypoints for a day hike—labeling and keeping track of them as you go along. Your receiver will also have a built-in map screen that you can tie into your waypoint list.

The coolest function of a GPS receiver is the "Goto" function. Your GPS can actually guide you to your destination using a steering screen. Other information connected to the Goto function includes whether you're on course, how much you have to correct your course, what your speed is, and how long it should take you to arrive at your destination.

Remember the problem with using a compass and having to correct for an area's declination? You can set your GPS receiver to either magnetic or true north. If you're using your GPS in conjunction with a map of the area, you might want to set it to true north so that it is in harmony with your map. But, if you're also

WORDS TO KNOW

waypoint: *a significant point on a journey, where the traveler can stop or change course.*

using a compass that you haven't automatically corrected for declination, you might want to set the GPS unit for magnetic north so your compass bearings and your GPS bearings are in synch. You can certainly switch back and forth between functions—just remember which one you're using.

Whenever you're navigating by GPS, you need to remember that, as with any piece of equipment, things can go wrong. The batteries could run low or run out (pack an extra set); you could have a hard time getting a reading from the satellites; you could lose your receiver or damage it; and/ or it could get wet. The point is, it's not smart to rely on this one piece of equipment for all of your navigational needs. You need to have a backup plan, and the tools to implement it.

You've learned how to use a topographic map and a compass. Bring them along and get used to plotting the coordinates you take by GPS on the map. Use your compass to test whether the compass readings you take match those recorded by GPS. Plot your route on the map—use both UTM coordinates and latitude and longitude coordinates to see how closely they correspond. Before you use the map with the GPS unit, remember to check all of the settings on your receiver. Look for the map datum notated along the bottom edge of your map (this is the reference point your map was drawn from—probably something like North American Datum 1927 or NAD 27). Select the units by deciding whether you're going to be using nautical miles or statute (land) miles. Check which kind of coordinates you'll be using—UTM or latitude and longitude. Set your receiver to either true north or magnetic north—particularly important when you coordinate your readings with those taken from a compass, which you know measures magnetic north. And make sure WAAS is turned on for increased accuracy.

Conclusion

In this book we've traveled across time from the Ice Age to the Space Age and across geography from Micronesia to Africa. On our journey we've not only learned about the history and science of navigation, we've also learned how to apply some of those principles so that we can find our own way in the world.

You should be able to read a map of the world and understand the importance

<blockquote>
ACTIVITY

Going on a Treasure Hunt with GPS

This will test your GPS skills and is fun to boot.

Supplies:

- GPS unit
- Internet access
- Notebook
- Pencil
- Something to leave in a cache

- Log onto www.geocaching.com and read about the sport of finding hidden treasures using your GPS unit. Read the FAQ section in "getting started." Back on the homepage, type your zip code into the search engine to find geocaches hidden near you. Here's one of the entries the author found. This cache is called "Barrel of Monkeys."

Difficulty: ★★★   Terrain: ★★★

This cache is hidden in the Cornell University Natural Area known as Monkey Run. The path is a part of the Cayuga Trails club system and Cornell's Plantations. It runs along both sides of Fall Creek and there are some beautiful vistas to enjoy along the way. The paths can be muddy in spots, and the woods are buggy in summer.
</blockquote>

Name five types of information that a GPS unit can give you.

of latitude and longitude. You should also be able to read a road map and a topographic map so that you can not only find your way to the next state but can also understand the kinds of hills and valleys you'll encounter if you decide to take a hike in a wilderness area. You can use these skills—of reading maps, of using a compass, of understanding a GPS unit—for the rest of your life.

So the next time you take a trip, take along a map and maybe even a compass or a GPS unit and have fun!

There are two approaches to the cache:

A) Park at N 42°28.305' W 076°25.835', just off Hwy 13 on Hanshaw Rd. From here you'll walk about 0.5 mile to reach the cache. You can go most all the way on main paths, the incline is only moderate, with only a little bushwhacking at the end. **It is this route that is rated above as 2.5 terrain, and it is appropriate for kids and dogs.**

B) Park at N 42°27.789' W 076° 25.628' at the end of Monkey Run Road just off Hwy 366. You can park in the areas marked as "snowplow turnaround" when there is no snow to be plowed. You'll approach the cache from the south instead of the north. By this route you'll walk only about 0.25 mile, but you must cross over the I-beams of an abandoned bridge (N 42°27.897' W 076°25.620'). This requires hoisting oneself up onto the bridge, and balancing or scooting across the foot-wide I-beams. **A fairly strenuous feat, it is not recommended for small children or those not athletically inclined.** Dogs would not be able to cross the bridge, but they could swim/wade across if the creek is not running too fast (as could a person).

The cache is in a large ammo box. It started out filled with a barrel of monkeys (take a monkey not the whole barrel!).

Find a cache near you and start to have fun!!

GEOCACHING

Geocaching (pronounced GEO—as in geography—CASHING—as in a hiding place or something hidden) is a really fun activity or game that has developed since GPS units came on the scene. It's like a modern-day treasure hunt. Objects are hidden and then the coordinates are sent to a geocache web site (like geocaching.com). Say you're going to visit Central New York State with your family. You could go to the web site and find out where geocaches are in that area. Or you can find out where geocaches are hidden near your home.

Geocaching map.

Sounds easy. What could be so difficult? You've got the coordinates, you've got a GPS unit, you've got a map, so it seems like you could just plug in the coordinates and go. But it's not so simple. Once you get to the site, you still have to find the treasure, which is often very cleverly hidden. There are very simple rules: you can take something from the cache, but you have to leave something in its place. Then you have to write about it in the logbook.

What's in a cache? A cache always has a logbook, which is left by the "founder" of the cache (the person who puts it there in the first place). A logbook can contain information about the cache, about nearby caches, jokes, or even clues or coordinates about caches that aren't published on the Internet. Visitors to the cache then sign the logbook. Many cache founders put their treasures in a waterproof plastic bucket. In addition to the logbook, the bucket/cache might contain CDs, videos, pictures, money, jewelry, games, and so forth. It's common to find the individual items placed in ziplock plastic bags to protect them. Remember the rule—if you take something from a cache, you have to leave something in return.

One neat thing that's developed since geocaching began is the "hitchhiker." This is an object in a cache that's supposed to be moved from cache to cache and then recorded in the logbook and online.

GLOSSARY

astrolabe: an instrument used to calculate latitude.

BCE: refers to before the common era, a modern term for BC.

bearing: a direction or a path.

CE: refers to common era, a modern term for AD.

celestial: relating to the stars.

chronometer: a very accurate portable clock used to determine longitude.

Clovis points: spear points found near Clovis, New Mexico.

conformal maps: preserves both the angles and shapes of small figures.

contour lines: curves that connect continuous points of the same altitude.

coordinates: numbers that identify a position.

declination: comparable to latitude, measured in degrees north of the equator.

degrees: one minute equals one nautical mile and 60 minutes equals one degree.

equal-area map: the scale remains the same anywhere on the map

Greenwich mean time: the local time at 0 degrees longitude, the prime meridian.

inertial guidance: guidance of an aircraft or spaceship using the instruments that measure direction and speed and a computer to maintain a predetermined course.

International Date Line: an imaginary north-south line at approximately 180 degrees in the Pacific Ocean; where each calendar day begins.

land mile: 5,280 feet

latitude: east-west parallel lines that encircle the earth north and south of the equator.

longitude: north-south lines that converge at the North and South Poles, and are measured in degrees east and west of the prime meridian.

magnetic deviation: the error of a compass due to local magnetic disturbances.

nautical mile: a mile at sea, measures approximately 6,080 feet

nautical: relating to the sea.

planimetric map: shows the horizontal position features. Sometimes called a line map.

prime meridian: the starting point for reckoning longitude at Greenwich, England.

sextant: an instrument used to measure how high the sun is above the horizon. The angle and the time it is measured can be used to calculate latitude.

summer solstice: when the sun is at its farthest point from the equator, in the Northern Hemisphere on June 21.

topographic map: represents both horizontal and vertical features, either with contour lines or spot elevations. Also called contour maps.

Universal Transverse Mercator: a geometric coordinate that is an alternative to using latitudes and longitudes. Measurements are in meters rather than degrees.

waypoint: a significant point on a journey where the traveler can stop or change course.

zenith: the highest point reached in the heavens by the sun, moon, or a star.

RESOURCES

Adult's Books

Fritz, Jean. *Around the World in a Hundred Years: From Henry the Navigator to Magellan*, Putnam, 1998

Gurney, Alan. *Compass: A Story of Exploration and Innovation* (W.W. Norton & Co., 2004).

Horwitz, Tony. *Blue Latitudes: Boldly going where Captain Cook has Gone Before* (Henry Holt & Company LLC, 2002).

Kjellstrom, Bjorn. *Be Expert with Map & Compass: The Complete Orienteering Handbook* (Hungry Minds, Inc., 1994).

Letham, Lawrence. *GPS Made Easy: Using Global Positioning Systems in the Outdoors, 4th ed.* (The Mountaineers, 2003).

Severin, Tim. *The China Voyage: Across the Pacific by Bamboo Raft* (London: Little, Brown, 1994).

Severin, Tim. *Tracking Marco Polo* (Peter Bedrick Books, 1986).

Sherman, Eric. *Geocaching: Hike and Seek with your GPS* (Apress, 2004).

Wilford, John Noble. *The Mapmakers: The story of the great pioneers in cartography—from Antiquity to the Space Age* (New York: Alfred A. Knopf, 1981).

Children's Books

Armstrong, Jennifer. *Shipwreck at the Bottom of the World : The Extraordinary True Story of Shackleton and the Endurance*, (Crown Books for Young Readers, 2000).

Harmon, Daniel. *Robert Peary: And the Quest for the North Pole* (Chelsea House Publications, 2001).

Herbert, Janis. *Lewis and Clark for Kids: Their Journey of Discovery With 21 Activities.* (Chicago Review Press, 2000).

Johnson, Sylvia. *Mapping the World.* (Atheneum, 1999).

MacDonald, Fiona. *Marco Polo: A Journey Through China* (Franklin Watts, 1998).

Matthews, Rupert. *Explorer* (DK Children, 2005).

Stott, Carole, and Gorton, Steve. *Space Exploration* (DK Children, 2004).

Web Sites

www.geocaching.com
www.eduscapes.com/geocaching/kids.htm
www.pbs.org/wgbh/nova/longitude
www.trimble.com/gps/
www.boatsafe.com/kids/navigation.htm
www.usgs.gov
www.21stcenturysciencetech.com/articles/fall01/navigators/navigators.html
www.asij.ac.jp/elementary/links/currlink/exploration.htm
www.celestialnavigation.net
www.polarization.com
www.lewis-clark.org
www.silk-road.com
www.nationalgeographic.com/xpeditions

INDEX